# SIMULATION for WORD PROCESSING
## Par Fore

**Mary Alice Eisch**
Larsen, Wisconsin

**Judith S. Voiers**
Weeki Wachee, Florida

**JOIN US ON THE INTERNET**
WWW: http://www.thomson.com    A service of I(T)P

**South-Western Educational Publishing**
*an International Thomson Publishing company* I(T)P

Cincinnati • Albany, NY • Belmont, CA • Bonn • Boston • Detroit • Johannesburg • London • Madrid
Melbourne • Mexico City • New York • Paris • Singapore • Tokyo • Toronto • Washington

Copyright © 1999
by SOUTH-WESTERN EDUCATIONAL PUBLISHING
Cincinnati, Ohio

**ALL RIGHTS RESERVED**

The text of this publication, or any part thereof, may not be reproduced or transmitted in any form or by any means, electronic or mechanical, including photocopying, recording, storage in an information retrieval system, or otherwise, without the prior written permission of the publisher.

ISBN: 0-538-68767-3

1 2 3 4 5 6 7 8 9 10 MZ 07 06 05 04 03 02 01 00 99 98
Printed in the United States of America

I(T)P®

International Thomson Publishing

South-Western Educational Publishing is a division of International Thomson Publishing Inc. The ITP logo is a registered trademark used herein under License by South-Western Educational Publishing.

*Managing Editor*: Carol Volz
*Project Manager*: Anne Noschang
*Design Coordinator*: Mike Broussard

# Table of Contents

| | |
|---|---|
| Introduction . . . . . . . . . . . . . . . . . . . . . . . . . 1 | |
| General Information . . . . . . . . . . . . . . . . . . . 1 | |

**February**
- Job 1—Create Letterheads . . . . . . . . . . . 3
- Job 2—Preparing the List of Members . . . 4
- Job 3—Mailing to Members . . . . . . . . . . 4
- Job 4—Payroll Sheets . . . . . . . . . . . . . . 4
- Job 5—Closeout Sheet (Part 1) . . . . . . . 5
- Job 6—Closeout Sheet (Part 2) . . . . . . . 5
- Job 7—Parking Sign . . . . . . . . . . . . . . . 5
- Job 8—Special Event Prize List . . . . . . . 5
- Job 9—Payroll Sheet . . . . . . . . . . . . . . . 5
- Job 10—Weekly Payroll Sheet . . . . . . . . 5
- Job 11—Address Book . . . . . . . . . . . . . 6
- Job 12—Hole-in-One . . . . . . . . . . . . . . . 6
- Job 13—Function Sheet . . . . . . . . . . . . 6
- Job 14—Cart Maintenance Forms . . . . . . 6
- Job 15—Payroll Sheet . . . . . . . . . . . . . . 6

**March**
- Job 16—Check Request . . . . . . . . . . . . 6
- Job 17—Handbook: Rules of Play . . . . . . 7
- Job 18—Function Sheet for Luncheon . . . 7
- Job 19—Inventory of Pro Shop . . . . . . . . 8
- Job 20—Payroll Sheet . . . . . . . . . . . . . . 8
- Job 21—Handbook: Bylaws . . . . . . . . . . 8
- Job 22—Handbook: League Events . . . . . 9
- Job 23—Handbook: Tournament Policies  9
- Job 24—Par Fore Weekly Schedule . . . . . 9
- Job 25—List of Members . . . . . . . . . . . . 9
- Job 26—Payroll Sheet . . . . . . . . . . . . . 10
- Job 27—Inventory . . . . . . . . . . . . . . . . 10

**April**
- Job 28—Club Advertisement . . . . . . . . 10
- Job 29—Membership List . . . . . . . . . . 10
- Job 30—Name Badges . . . . . . . . . . . . 10
- Job 31—Request for Reimbursement . . 11
- Job 32—Payroll Sheet . . . . . . . . . . . . . 11
- Job 33—Inventory . . . . . . . . . . . . . . . . 11
- Job 34—Petty Cash Request . . . . . . . . 11
- Job 35—Changes to Member Account . . 11
- Job 36—Petty Cash . . . . . . . . . . . . . . . 12
- Job 37—18-Hole Invitational Notice . . . . 12
- Job 38—Payroll Sheet . . . . . . . . . . . . . 12
- Job 39—Inventory . . . . . . . . . . . . . . . . 12

**May**
- Job 40—Weekly Sign-ups . . . . . . . . . . 12
- Job 41—Board Meeting Agenda . . . . . . 12
- Job 42—Invitational Budget . . . . . . . . . 12
- Job 43—Payroll Sheet . . . . . . . . . . . . . 13
- Job 44—Inventory . . . . . . . . . . . . . . . . 13
- Job 45—Minutes . . . . . . . . . . . . . . . . . 13
- Job 46—Hole-in-One . . . . . . . . . . . . . . 13

- Job 47—Tournament Sign-up Sheets . . 13
- Job 48—Mailing to Golf Clubs . . . . . . . . 14
- Job 49—Handicap Conversion Chart . . . 14
- Job 50—Payroll Sheet . . . . . . . . . . . . . 14
- Job 51—Inventory . . . . . . . . . . . . . . . . 14

**June**
- Job 52—Weekly Sign-ups . . . . . . . . . . 14
- Job 53—Petty Cash . . . . . . . . . . . . . . . 14
- Job 54—Slow Play . . . . . . . . . . . . . . . 14
- Job 55—Checklist for Tournament . . . . 15
- Job 56—Letter to Tournament Sponsors  15
- Job 57—Invitational Deadline Poster . . . 15
- Job 58—Details with Pro Shop Staff . . . . 15
- Job 59—Payroll Sheet . . . . . . . . . . . . . 15
- Job 60—Inventory . . . . . . . . . . . . . . . . 15
- Job 61—Slow Play Letter . . . . . . . . . . . 15
- Job 62—Change to Member Account . . . 16
- Job 63—Notice . . . . . . . . . . . . . . . . . . 16
- Job 64—Tournament List . . . . . . . . . . . 16
- Job 65—Check Request . . . . . . . . . . . 16
- Job 66—Order Favors and Prizes . . . . . 16
- Job 67—List for Bulletin Board . . . . . . . 16
- Job 68—Function Sheet . . . . . . . . . . . 17
- Job 69—Tournament Information . . . . . 17
- Job 70—Reimbursement Request . . . . 17
- Job 71—Hole-in-One . . . . . . . . . . . . . . 17
- Job 72—Volunteer Sign-up Sheet . . . . . 17
- Job 73—Payroll Sheet . . . . . . . . . . . . . 17
- Job 74—Inventory . . . . . . . . . . . . . . . . 17

**July**
- Job 75—Weekly Sign-ups . . . . . . . . . . 17
- Job 76—Name Badges . . . . . . . . . . . . 18
- Job 77—Signs . . . . . . . . . . . . . . . . . . 18
- Job 78—Pin Placement Sheet . . . . . . . 18
- Job 79—Winners' List . . . . . . . . . . . . . 18
- Job 80—Certificates for Winners . . . . . . 18
- Job 81—Board Meeting Agenda . . . . . . 18
- Job 82—Tournament Accounting . . . . . 18
- Job 83—Minutes of Board Meeting . . . . 18
- Job 84—Payroll Sheet . . . . . . . . . . . . . 19
- Job 85—Inventory . . . . . . . . . . . . . . . . 19
- Job 86—Change to Member Account . . . 19
- Job 87—Invitational Thank You Letters . 19
- Job 88—Hole-in-One . . . . . . . . . . . . . . 19
- Job 89—Payroll Sheet . . . . . . . . . . . . . 19
- Job 90—Inventory . . . . . . . . . . . . . . . . 19

# Progress Record

Name _____

| | Printed | Score | Date Completed | Instructor |
|---|---|---|---|---|

**February**
- Job 1—Create Letterheads — ---
- Job 2—Preparing the List of Members — ---
- Job 3—Mailing to Members — 2 pgs.
- Job 4—Payroll Sheets — ......
- Job 5—Closeout Sheet (Part 1) — ......
- Job 6—Closeout Sheet (Part 2) — ......
- Job 7—Parking Sign — ......
- Job 8—Special Event Prize List — ......
- Job 9—Payroll Sheet — ......
- Job 10—Weekly Payroll Sheet — ......
- Job 11—Address Book — ---
- Job 12—Hole-in-One — ......
- Job 13—Function Sheet — ......
- Job 14—Cart Maintenance Forms — ......
- Job 15—Payroll Sheet — ......

**March**
- Job 16—Check Request — ......
- Job 17—Handbook: Rules of Play — ......
- Job 18—Function Sheet for Luncheon — ......
- Job 19—Inventory of Pro Shop — ......
- Job 20—Payroll Sheet — ......
- Job 21—Handbook: Bylaws — 4 pgs.
- Job 22—Handbook: League Events — ......
- Job 23—Handbook: Tournament Policies — 7 pgs.
- Job 24—Par Fore Weekly Schedule — 4 pgs.
- Job 25—List of Members — ---
- Job 26—Payroll Sheet — ......
- Job 27—Inventory — ......

**April**
- Job 28—Club Advertisement — ......
- Job 29—Membership List — 4 pgs.
- Job 30—Name Badges — 7 pgs.
- Job 31—Request for Reimbursement — ......
- Job 32—Payroll Sheet — 2 pgs.
- Job 33—Inventory — ......
- Job 34—Petty Cash Request — ......
- Job 35—Changes to Member Account — ......
- Job 36—Petty Cash — ......
- Job 37—18-Hole Invitational Notice — ......
- Job 38—Payroll Sheet — ......
- Job 39—Inventory — ......

**May**
- Job 40—Weekly Sign-ups — 4 pgs.
- Job 41—Board Meeting Agenda — ......
- Job 42—Invitational Budget — ......
- Job 43—Payroll Sheet — ......
- Job 44—Inventory — ......

Name _____

|  | Printed | Score | Date Completed | Instructor |
|---|---|---|---|---|
| Job 45—Minutes | 2 pgs. | | | |
| Job 46—Hole-in-One | ...... | | | |
| Job 47—Tournament Sign-up Sheets | 3 pgs. | | | |
| Job 48—Mailing to Golf Clubs | ...... | | | |
| Job 49—Handicap Conversion Chart | ...... | | | |
| Job 50—Payroll Sheet | ...... | | | |
| Job 51—Inventory | ...... | | | |
| **June** | | | | |
| Job 52—Weekly Sign-ups | 4 pgs. | | | |
| Job 53—Petty Cash | ...... | | | |
| Job 54—Slow Play | 2 pgs. | | | |
| Job 55—Checklist for Tournament | ...... | | | |
| Job 56—Letter to Tournament Sponsors | ...... | | | |
| Job 57—Invitational Deadline Poster | ...... | | | |
| Job 58—Details with Pro Shop Staff | ...... | | | |
| Job 59—Payroll Sheet | ...... | | | |
| Job 60—Inventory | ...... | | | |
| Job 61—Slow Play Letter | ...... | | | |
| Job 62—Change to Member Account | ...... | | | |
| Job 63—Notice | ...... | | | |
| Job 64—Tournament List | 4 pgs. | | | |
| Job 65—Check Request | ...... | | | |
| Job 66—Order Favors and Prizes | ...... | | | |
| Job 67—List for Bulletin Board | ...... | | | |
| Job 68—Function Sheet | ...... | | | |
| Job 69—Tournament Information | ...... | | | |
| Job 70—Reimbursement Request | ...... | | | |
| Job 71—Hole-in-One | ...... | | | |
| Job 72—Volunteer Sign-up Sheet | ...... | | | |
| Job 73—Payroll Sheet | ...... | | | |
| Job 74—Inventory | ...... | | | |
| **July** | | | | |
| Job 75—Weekly Sign-ups | 11 pgs. | | | |
| Job 76—Name Badges | ...... | | | |
| Job 77—Signs | 5 pgs. | | | |
| Job 78—Pin Placement Sheet | 2 pgs. | | | |
| Job 79—Winners' List | ...... | | | |
| Job 80—Certificates for Winners | 8 pgs. | | | |
| Job 81—Board Meeting Agenda | ...... | | | |
| Job 82—Tournament Accounting | ...... | | | |
| Job 83—Minutes of Board Meeting | 2 pgs. | | | |
| Job 84—Payroll Sheet | ...... | | | |
| Job 85—Inventory | ...... | | | |
| Job 86—Change to Member Account | ...... | | | |
| Job 87—Invitational Thank You Letters | 2 pgs. | | | |
| Job 88—Hole-in-One | ...... | | | |
| Job 89—Payroll Sheet | ...... | | | |
| Job 90—Inventory | ...... | | | |

# SIMULATION FOR WORD PROCESSING: PAR FORE

## *INTRODUCTION*

Welcome to the Ohio River Golf Club located in Cincinnati, Ohio. You have just been hired as an assistant to the two golf professionals who manage the entire golfing program, including the Pro Shop for the club. Your responsibility is to handle a variety of word processing jobs for the Pro Shop staff.

Most of your work will be related to the Par Fore Golf League that is scheduled to play every Tuesday afternoon from April through September. The league consists of 24 two-person teams and six alternates. All members have an established United States Golf Association (USGA) handicap which is used to "even out" the competition among the golfers with varying degrees of skill.

Although league play for the golfing season doesn't begin until April, your tasks will begin in February. For six months, you will be responsible for such tasks as:
- maintaining the league's membership list
- preparing mailings to members
- updating, formatting, and editing the league handbook
- creating documents and forms for league events, such as luncheons and tournaments
- creating documents related to meetings of the league board of directors, such as an agenda, minutes, and financial statements
- maintaining the Pro Shop inventory
- creating advertisements
- creating employee-related forms and documents

# GENERAL INFORMATION

Your work will be coming from the golf professionals at the Ohio River Golf Club and the Par Fore league officers. You'll also be working closely with the Pro Shop clerks.

| Golf Professionals | Pro Shop Clerks | League Officers |
|---|---|---|
| Scott Alexejun | Barbara Telander | Barb Krull, President |
| Jason Jarosik | Janie Hodges | Don Ihlenfeld, Secretary |
| | Gene Shultz | Margaret Dobbe, Treasurer |

### Saving Your Documents

You will be creating and saving quite a number of documents in your work at the golf club. Your instructions for saving will assume that the completed documents will be saved on a diskette in Drive A of your computer (the **solutions** disk). If your instructor would like you to save your work in a different location, you will be given that information.

You will probably wish to name most of your completed documents by job (e.g., **job34**). In the case of data files or form documents that you'll use more than once, a more descriptive name is recommended. The instructions for some jobs will give specific information about naming your files.

### Letters

You will be creating a wide variety of documents, including letters—many using merge. You'll also use the template feature in your word processing program to create the letterhead format for those letters. Study the letter at the right to see how your letters should look.

- All letters should be prepared in block style on the league or golf club letterhead.
- If possible, use a proportional sans serif font.
- The date should be a double space below the letterhead, and it should be followed by at least a quadruple space. In the case of very short letters, adjust the position of the letter on the page by leaving more space between the date and the inside address.
- Use one-inch margins.
- Put a colon after the greeting and a comma after the closing.

The assumption is that you will be using a #10 envelope (9.5" x 4"). If possible (depending on your printing capabilities), prepare an envelope for each letter. Use paper cut to size for the envelopes or print them on the backs of the appropriate letters.

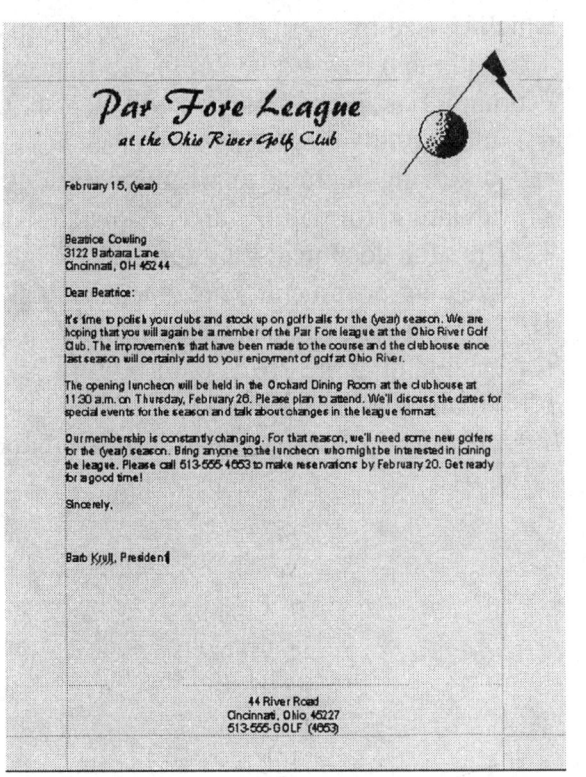

*Suggested Letter Layout*

The text for the return address for the league is illustrated at the right. Drop the first line when you are sending letters for the golf club. Check with your instructor to see if you may keep the return addresses in the address book on your computer for the times you'll be needing them.

If you can't do envelopes at all because of printer limitations, prepare labels for the large mailings and skip the envelopes for the single letters.

> Par Fore League
> Ohio River Golf Club
> 44 River Road
> Cincinnati, OH 45227
> 513-555-GOLF (4653)

Return Address for Envelopes

### Other Documents

Dozens of the documents are one-of-a-kind documents. Many of your jobs will include the preparation of forms for use by the league and Pro Shop staff. Some of those forms will require calculations, giving you an opportunity to use formulas in your tables. Keep in mind as you create the forms that you will probably be expected to fill in the blanks on some of them. Some of them should be prepared as keyboard merge (form fill or stop code) documents, where you key the needed information into the document during the merge. (Note that these will always be referred to as *keyboard merge* documents.) Create all forms in such a way that you won't struggle later on when you are expected to complete them. If you find when using the forms that they don't work well, redesign them so the required information can be entered efficiently.

One of your jobs will be to update the league handbook. If your word processing program has booklet printing capabilities, prepare the handbook in booklet format. In many cases you'll be shown an image of the document. Your job will be to use the available tools to prepare a similar document.

### General

Use the current year for all jobs. Many of them show *(year)* where you should fill in the year. In situations where you are doing work for a specific date, a description of that date (i.e., first Tuesday in April) will show in parentheses. Fill in the appropriate information so each document is properly dated.

If you haven't already done so, develop the habit of checking all work for errors before printing. Many of the documents with which you will work were prepared by volunteers and contain errors. You'll be able to find some of those errors using your software spelling checker. Others will have to be detected by careful proofreading.

Also, you should develop the habit of checking each document for attractive formatting before printing. That involves looking for single lines of a paragraph or section that shouldn't be alone on a page of a multiple-page document and using the appropriate software commands to keep text together. It also involves placement of shorter a document on the page.

Although many of the jobs listed for February are jobs that have needed to be done for some time, your work will be divided into months and jobs. The jobs are numbered consecutively to make them easier to track. The monthly job instructions follow this introductory material. The source documents needed for the jobs begin on page 20. Be sure to read the job instructions thoroughly and study any source documents before beginning each job.

# JOB NARRATIVE

## FEBRUARY

### Job 1—Create Letterheads

Your first job is to create a letterhead for the Ohio River Golf Club that is customized for the Par Fore league. As part of the letterhead, you need a graphics image of some kind to be used as the logo. If you wish, you can make the two logos almost alike—with a very small distinction (perhaps the color) to separate the league logo from the club logo.

Look at the logo for the Par Fore league in the sample letter on page 2. Note that it is simply a circle that is "shaded" to look like a golf ball. Within it is a diagonal line and a triangle to look like the flag from a golf green. To use a logo such as this one and make the Ohio River logo different from the Par Fore logo, you could change the color of the flag or the number on the flag.

You may use any kind of golf image that comes with the text processing program you are using, you may find a golf image in any clip art you have in the classroom or at home, you could find an image you like in a magazine or newspaper and scan it (if your classroom has a scanner), or you may try your hand at creating a logo with circles, triangles and lines.

Copy both logo images to your **solutions** disk so you can access them from that source for other applications. Name them **clublogo** and **forelogo** so you can find them when you need them.

When the logos are created, create the letterheads incorporating those logos. Use templates for the letterheads, so you don't have to worry about the parts moving around when you're using the letterheads. If you can create both letterheads in one template, do it that way so the letter parts are kept together. Save the template as **Letterheads** on your **solutions** disk so you can find the file easily.

For the club letterhead, include the name of the club at the top and the address and phone number in a footer at the bottom of the page. For the league letterhead, include the name of the league, followed by the name of the club in smaller letters. Include the address and phone number (the same as for the club) in a footer at the bottom of the page.

### Job 2—Preparing the List of Members

The official opening of the golfing season is only two months away. You need to send out a letter to last year's members of the Par Fore league announcing the Opening Day Luncheon. Last year's membership was saved in a program that is incompatible with your program, so you will need to key the names, addresses, and phone numbers of all 54 members of the league.

| first name |
| last name |
| street |
| city |
| state |
| zip |
| phone |

Key the information as a data source or data file so it can be used to merge with a variety of form documents. Use the data fields listed in the box. When you have entered the data for all members, proofread carefully and save the file with your solutions as **Fore**.

### Job 3—Mailing to Members

You've been given a copy of last year's letter. Use the league letterhead and key it as a form document so it can be merged with the data source you just prepared. Use the first Tuesday in February as the date of the letter. A number of changes need to be made in the letter as you key:

- Change the date of the luncheon to the first Tuesday in April. Be sure to change the year in the first sentence to the current year.
- Change the location of the luncheon to the newly remodeled dining room at Ohio River.
- At the closing luncheon at the end of the last season, the league decided to change its name from *Bogey Buddies* to *Par Fore*. It made the group sound more sophisticated.
- Put the letter on the first page and the reservation form on the second page. Change the wording in the letter to reflect that change.

Save the letter as **opening job3** and perform the merge, making envelopes at the same time you merge. Print the final three letters and the final three envelopes. Close all documents without saving.

## *Job 4—Payroll Sheets*

The Ohio River Golf Club has a poor system of keeping track of the hours worked by employees. You have volunteered to make a payroll sheet similar to one you saw at a different company for the employees to try. A miniature of the sample payroll sheet is illustrated. The Ohio River pay period begins on Saturday, not Wednesday. Can you create one that is similar or better? Turn the paper to landscape and create two identical forms beside one another on a page.

## *Job 5—Closeout Sheet (Part 1)*

The Club has also been using the same format for daily cash closeouts for some time, but they write everything by hand. You've explained that if you prepare a form where they can write the needed information in the blanks, they will be able to complete the job in much less time. Prepare the form using landscape orientation. Prepare two forms to a page so the paper can be cut in half. At the end of the form, add the following paragraph:

**The end-of-day work must be balanced before forwarding to accounting. When an error is located, the ticket(s) that caused the problem must be photocopied and placed for correction by accounting.**

## *Job 6—Closeout Sheet (Part 2)*

The information that is entered on the closeout sheet by hand must eventually be entered into the computer. Some employees would rather key the information directly into the computer and key their names in the signature location and initial the signature. You can help this process by making the form into a keyboard merge. Convert the form you just completed by removing the lines for the amounts and inserting keyboard merge codes. Remove the form at the right, so only the left half of the paper will be used. (The blank half sheet can be used as scrap paper.)

## *Job 7—Parking Sign*

The club has had a problem with people parking in the service area. Please prepare a sign for that area. Use landscape orientation and as much of the page as you can. Make the sign attractive and easy to read.

## *Job 8—Special Event Prize List*

Create the weekly prize list sheet. Fill the sheet with prize information blanks.

*Job 9—Payroll Sheet*

You have been asked to take over some of the payroll responsibilities for hourly employees. You were amazed at the obsolete procedure being used, so you decided to prepare a form that could be completed on the computer each week when the hours were submitted. Create a keyboard merge form that multiplies the overtime hours times 1½, totals the hours, and multiplies the total hours times the rate of pay. The club treasurer will prepare the checks for all employees.

*Job 10—Weekly Payroll Sheet*

The payroll week always ends on Friday. Prepare the payroll sheet for the end of the second week in February. You'll be preparing the payroll sheet each second and fourth Friday. Whoever works in the Pro Shop late on Fridays will prepare the payroll sheet on the first and third Fridays.

*Job 11—Address Book*

Your boss has decided that the best way to keep the information about the employees of Ohio River Golf Club is in an Address Book. In that way, phone calls can be made directly from the book, and addresses for occasional correspondence can also be easily accessed. Please create personal entries for the Pro Shop clerks and the golf professionals.

Locate the addresses of the three Par Fore league officers and add them to your address book, too. Save your address book as **ORemploy**.

*Job 12—Hole-in-One*

Occasionally, a player makes a "hole-in-one." This is quite an accomplishment! The Ohio River Golf Club has a procedure to recognize players who make a hole-in-one by printing the information in the newsletter, the local newspaper, adding the player's name on a plaque in the hallway, etc.

Create a keyboard merge form for filling in the critical information about the hole-in-one and providing a checklist to make sure the Pro Shop employees take care of the duties involved. Use Ohio River letterhead for the form and save it as **Hole-in-One**.

*Job 13—Function Sheet*

Ohio River Golf Club needs a new function sheet to be used for planning events such as the Par Fore Opening Day Luncheon. Use the club letterhead, and prepare a form that can be filled out by hand or on the computer. Create the form in any way you wish. Make it look good, and make it easy to use. It MUST fit on one page.

*Job 14—Cart Maintenance Forms*

Scott Alexejun in the Pro Shop has asked you to prepare cart maintenance tickets for the golf carts. He has shown you a sample that he likes from a different club. Prepare the forms to be printed four to a page. Include the name of the golf club and the club logo.

*Job 15—Payroll Sheet*

Prepare the payroll sheet for the fourth Friday in February.

# MARCH

## Job 16—Check Request

The committee members planning the opening day luncheon of the Par Fore Golf League have
decorations and door prizes. When a request is made for a check not
or receipt, a check request form must be prepared. The old form wasn't
ase use the letterhead and prepare the form to be filled out by hand.

*f Play*

weeks you will be working on the handbook for the Par Fore Golf
rts are finished, you will assemble the handbook and print it for
ncheon.
dbook, and the *Rules of Play* portion of the handbook needs revision.
ons disk named **Handbook**. Key this document and save it as **Rules**
it the document as you work. (Read through the entire list before
portion of the document extends to a second page.
quarter-inch indents for all parts of the handbook.
*dded Ball* item, number the eight items that begin at the left margin.
argin. Indent following the numeral so the text is aligned like these
b 17. Use bullets for the two major categories under *Relief*. Use a
or the items listed within those major categories.
*alties* is the first item. Move *Free Drop* so it is just above *Relief*.
n to a half inch to make room for a footnote. Then add a footnote at
the end of the "Please read . . ." statement at the top of the document. The footnote should read
as follows:

> *1998 Rules of Golf, And The Rules of Amateur Status*, THE UNITED STATES
> GOLF ASSOCIATION and THE ROYAL AND ANCIENT GOLF CLUB OF ST.
> ANDREWS, SCOTLAND.

5. Look for the term *proshop* and change it to *Pro Shop*. This term has been keyed as one word throughout the handbook documents, and it should be two words.
6. Remove the underlining from the major sections and replace it with Bold.
7. Change the font size for the title of the document to 18 pt. bold.
8. Change *RULE* to *Rule* each time a USGA rule is referenced.

## Job 18—Function Sheet for Luncheon

It's the first Thursday in March, and the plans are well under way for the Par Fore League luncheon. Please fill out the function sheet. Margot Babcock is the chairperson for the event, and her fax number is 513-555-1402. Lynn Doell is helping, but she doesn't have a fax machine. You'd like round tables, set for 55 people. You need a podium, a microphone, a speaker's table, and a registration table. The colors for the banquet are green and yellow, and the committee is providing their own centerpieces. The luncheon will probably end by 2:30 p.m.

The lunch will be served buffet style. The menu should include cold cuts and hard rolls for the diners to make their own sandwiches ($4.20 per person). Also available should be platters of tomatoes, onions, and lettuce ($1.00 per person), and potato chips (50¢ per person). Coffee, hot tea, and iced tea should be served at the tables ($1.05 per person). The committee decided on fresh fruit for dessert ($1.50 per person). Gratuity is $1.75 per person. The cost for the luncheon can be calculated by multiplying the amount per person times the number of golfers expected to attend.

### *Job 19—Inventory of Pro Shop*

The Pro Shop at Ohio River Golf Club stocks many items. Some of them are seasonal or trendy items. Others are items that are continually in stock, such as a variety of golf clubs and golf clothing. The shop manages the inventory of the miscellaneous items on an as-needed basis. The regular items, however, need to be tracked weekly, and good records kept of those sales.

Use a table to create a form listing all of the items that are continually in stock. Key the stock codes, description, wholesale price, and retail price for each item. Then add formulas that calculate the percentage of markup, net income on items sold, and tax generated on the sale of the items. (Note that a different formula may be needed for the rows containing Club Rentals and Club Repair.) Add a row at the bottom for totals so you can total the Net Income column and the Tax Generated column. Work carefully when creating this form. Make it attractive, accurate, and easy to use. You will be using it often.

It is now the end of the second week in March. Open the inventory sheet and insert the quantities of items sold in the past week (they are listed by stock code). Calculate the net income and tax generated as well as the totals at the bottom.

You will be preparing this inventory sheet at the same time you are preparing the payroll sheets on the second and fourth Fridays. Whoever prepares the payroll sheets on the first and third Fridays will also prepare the weekly inventory sheets for those weeks.

### *Job 20—Payroll Sheet*

Prepare the payroll sheet for the second week in March. With the golfing season rapidly approaching, regular hours are being increased to 37 per week. Beginning in April, regular hours will be 40 hours per week.

### *Job 21—Handbook: Bylaws*

You learned earlier that the members of the league voted to change the name of the league from *Bogey Buddies* to *Par Fore*. As a result, the bylaws need to be updated. What's more, only a hard copy (on paper) of the bylaws can be found. You have the opportunity to key this lengthy document and correct it.

Repair the document as follows. When you finish, save it as **Bylaws** in the **Handbook** folder.
1. Replace *Bogey Buddies* with **Par Fore** in the title and in the first line of Article I. In parentheses following the word *League* insert **(PFGL)** as the acronym to identify the league. Replace all references to the league throughout the bylaws with **PFGL**.
2. Insert (ORGC) after the name of the club in the second line of Article I. Replace all references to the Ohio River Golf Club with **ORGC**.
3. Remove the underlines from the article sections. Format them with Bold and center each of them. Replace the "space-hyphen-space" between the article number and the name of the article with em dashes.

4. In Article VII, format the list of nine standing committees into three equal columns. In the section that describes the standing committees, format the name of each committee with italic. If necessary, reorganize the descriptions so they are in the same order as the three-column list.
5. Format the two title lines with a larger font size and bold, if you wish.
6. Add a footer that includes the name of the league at the left and the word *Page* followed by the page number at the right. Format the text of the footer with an 8-pt. sans serif font face.
7. Beginning on the first page, change the bottom margin to a half inch.
8. Insert the current date following *Revised* at the end.

### Job 22—Handbook: League Events

Time is short. It is almost time for the opening day luncheon, and the handbook must be finished. Key the document describing the league events, making any necessary corrections as you work. Format the underlined text with bold. Remove the colons and replace them with em dashes. Format the title the same as the title for the Rules of Play. Key carefully and proofread and save the file in your **Handbook** folder as **Events**.

### Job 23—Handbook: Tournament Policies

Key the file about tournament policies. Save it in your **Handbook** folder as **Tournament**. Format and edit it like the other handbook files, changing margins, tab stops, and the league name. Change all occurrences of *chairman* to *chairperson*. Don't forget to proofread.

Combine the four parts of the handbook into one large file and save it in the **Handbook** folder as **handbook**. Arrange the files in the following order: Bylaws, Rules, Events, Tournaments. Use Landscape Orientation, half-inch margins, and put two half-pages on each sheet of paper. Begin each file on a new "page." Prepare a title page for the handbook that uses the Par Fore logo and includes the names and phone numbers of the league officers. Check it over for appropriate page endings, page numbering (in the footer), and a generally attractive appearance. If your software allows you to print using the booklet printing option, prepare your handbook that way.

### Job 24—Par Fore Weekly Schedule

The schedule has been prepared for the weekly golf matches. Key the schedule and save it as **weekly schedule**, put it on league letterhead, and dress it up. You will be needing it for preparation of the sign-up sheets for the weekly tournaments, the first of which you are about to prepare.

A sign-up sheet is needed for the weekly tournaments. Key it on the league letterhead, make it lovely, and make it a form document with keyboard merge codes for the date and the tournament format. Making it a merge document allows you to easily enter the weekly information as you prepare the sheets for each week of the season. Save the file as **weekly sign-up**.

The sign-up sheets will be posted on the bulletin board a month at a time. Use the weekly schedule as a reference and keyboard merge to prepare the sign-up sheet for the first four weeks, beginning with the first Tuesday in April. Include the date and the type of tournament.

### Job 25—List of Members

Reservations have been received for the luncheon. Four members are unable to join the league this year, and members need to be added from the waiting list to fill their places. Open **Fore** from your **solutions** folder. Bring the list of league members up to date and save it as **ParFore**.

*Job 26—Payroll Sheet*

Prepare the payroll sheet for the fourth Friday in March. You've put in quite a few overtime hours with your work on the tournament handbook. Not only do you have the satisfaction of having prepared a great handbook, but now you'll receive extra pay, too.

*Job 27—Inventory*

March was a slow month for the Pro Shop. Complete the weekly inventory sheet for the fourth week of the month.

# APRIL

*Job 28—Club Advertisement*

With the golf season nearing, the management has decided to do some advertising in the local newspapers. Prepare a quarter-page advertisement for the club.

*Job 29—Membership List*

Barb has made the team assignments. Key the list of teams in an attractive format using columns so the document fits on one page. It will be distributed to the members at the luncheon. Then print it for reference and save it as **job29a**.

At this point, it looks as though most of the 48 members of the Par Fore league as well as the six alternates will be attending the opening day luncheon.

Open the **ParFore** data source and add the team assignments as follows:
1. Add a *team number* field.
2. Arrange the membership list in alphabetic order.
3. Go through the list, adding the appropriate team number to the record for each member of the league. (Key **Alt.** in the team number field for the alternate members.) Save the membership list again as **ParFore-T** (with **T**eams).
4. Merge the list into a table format with columns for the committee to check for payment received, attendance, and materials distributed. Save the merged table as **job29b**.

When the committee has used the table to check off who has paid for the luncheon and whether they attended, they will know who didn't get copies of the handbook and other materials handed out at the luncheon.

*Job 30—Name Badges*

Create a name badge form document to match your membership data file and enter field codes so the form can be merged with your **ParFore-T** data source. Use a white, eight-to-the-page name badge—Avery 5395 is fine if it is available. Center the first name in a large font size, and the last name in a smaller font size below the first name. Below the last name, center the word *Team* followed by the team number. Find a creative way to use the Par Fore logo to decorate the name badge. Save the form document as **badge**; you'll be using it again. Print the name badges but don't save the finished document.

## Job 31—Request for Reimbursement

Jason Jarosik has been doing some extra work for the golf club in addition to his regular Pro Shop duties. He has given some golfing lessons and has repaired some of the members' clubs. He discussed this with a friend of his from a neighboring club and came back with a form to use to request reimbursement for his activities. Create a similar form for use by the Ohio River Golf Club. See if you can make one that is more attractive and useful! Save the form as **reimbursement**.

Fill out a copy of the form for Jason. He gave a $35 lesson to member #23114 and to member #13764. He repaired two clubs for Member #23114 and three clubs for member #12197. Club repairs cost $5 each.

## Job 32—Payroll Sheet

Now that the golf season is in full swing, 40 hours is standard for the hourly employees. Jack Schwab has been hired as an additional part-time employee. Even with those changes, workers are expected to work overtime hours.

Open your payroll sheet document and add a row including Jack's information. Be sure the formulas are in place and resave the file. Use merge to record the hours for the second week in April.

Add Jack to the employee address book. He lives at 216A Bagdad Court, Cincinnati, OH 45230. His phone number is 513-555-7117.

Create a form document letter to include with the weekly paycheck for the full-time hourly employees. The letter should be merged with the hourly employees in the Address Book reminding the employees that beginning with this pay period, regular hours are increased to 40 per week. In the letter, introduce Jack as a new part-time employee who will be working 20 to 30 hours per week to help during the busy season. The letter should be prepared for Scott Alexejun's signature. Save the form document as **job32b**. Print all four letters (including yours). Do not save the merged letters.

## Job 33—Inventory

Prepare the inventory sheet for the second week in April.

## Job 34—Petty Cash Request

Since you seem do to such a good job of setting up forms, the Pro Shop staff members have suggested you replace the old, hand-written form being used by Ohio River for requesting petty cash. The suggested top and bottom of the form are illustrated. Give it a title that includes a place to fill in the current date, and make it fill a page. Add formulas that total the expenditures and subtract the total from the original petty cash balance. Save the form as **petty cash**.

## Job 35—Changes to Member Account

After signing up for a season of golfing and making their choices regarding carts, lockers, training fees, etc., members often change their minds about their needs. In the past, the club has bumbled through making the changes without any formal method. A form that can be used either to write the changes or to key them into the computer would be nice. Can you design one that fits on the club letterhead and is useful? Save the form as **member change**.

*Job Narrative*

### Job 36—Petty Cash

You completed the petty cash form just in time. It's the second Tuesday in April, and Scott Alexejun just returned from a trip to the store where he bought some necessary items for the Pro Shop. He took money from the petty cash fund for his purchases and gave you the sales slip. Use your petty cash form to record the information and show the new balance.

### Job 37—18-Hole Tournament Notice

Now that the season is getting under way, it is time to start planning for the sixth annual 18-hole invitational tournament to be hosted in July by the Par Fore Golf League. Members from a dozen local golf clubs are invited to attend, and the date has been set for the first Tuesday in July. An early notice needs to be sent to the clubs telling them the date of the tournament and that registration materials will be mailed shortly.

Key the names, addresses, and phone numbers of the clubs to be invited as a data source file, using the fields listed at in the box at the right. Save the file as **clubs**. Then create a short notice letter as a form document to be merged with **clubs**. The letter should be printed on Par Fore letterhead and sent to the attention of the Golf Association Chairperson at each club. Prepare the letters and envelopes for the letters. Print all of the letters and envelopes. Save the form letter as **job37**. Do not save the completed merge.

```
club name
street address
city, state zip
telephone
```

### Job 38—Payroll Sheet & Job 39—Inventory

Prepare the payroll sheets for the fourth Friday in April. Then prepare the weekly inventory sheet for the fourth Friday in April.

# MAY

### Job 40—Weekly Sign-ups

Prepare the weekly tournament sign-up sheets for May, just like you did for April. Remember to include the date and the type of tournament for each sheet.

### Job 41—Board Meeting Agenda

The board meeting of the Par Fore league will be held at 1 p.m. on the first Tuesday in May. Prepare the agenda on Par Fore letterhead. Space it attractively. Insert the names of the league officers in the appropriate places. The membership chairperson is Alex Holbrook, the rules chairperson is Don Ihlenfeld, the handicap chairperson is Dave Brantley, the tournament chairperson is Peggy Eick, and the invitational co-chairpersons are Florence Rogers and Lynn Doell.

### Job 42—Invitational Budget

Margaret Dobbe, league treasurer, has asked you to prepare the tournament budget for the board meeting. Use Par Fore letterhead for the budget. Use dot leaders, if possible, to join the columns.

### Job 43—Payroll Sheet & Job 44—Inventory

Prepare the payroll sheet for the second week in May.
Prepare the weekly inventory for the second week in May.

### Job 45—Minutes

The league secretary took minutes of the board meeting and has given you a rough draft. Create a two-column report of the board meeting, matching the agenda items with the information in the minutes. A suggested arrangement for the beginning of the minutes is illustrated in the source documents. Include "Respectfully submitted" followed by the signature of the secretary of the league at the bottom of the minutes, along with the date the minutes were prepared. Be sure to proofread for accuracy before printing.

### Job 46—Hole-in-One

On May (third Tuesday), Kay Koclanes shot a hole-in-one on Hole 11. The hole is 156 yards, she used a 3 iron, and the shot was witnessed by Beulah Seager, Sue Steiner, Lynn Doell. Use keyboard merge to fill out the top part of the *Hole-in-One* sheet. Print it so the Pro Shop staff can use the checklist at the bottom to follow the procedure that gives Kay all the attention she deserves for her accomplishment.

### Job 47—Tournament Sign-up Sheets

Two sign-up sheets need to be prepared for the invitational tournament. One will be be sent to the local clubs along with a letter of invitation. The other is for Par Fore members to sign up for the tournament. Use Par Fore letterhead for both sheets.

For the mailing to the clubs, key the information for the top of the form and provide sign-up lines for 8 members and 2 alternates. (You may use a table form, if you wish.) Be sure to include a place for the players to indicate their handicaps, their handicap index, whether they need a cart, and what they would like for lunch. At the bottom, create a signature line for the club's golf professional for handicap verification.

Make a copy of the sign-up sheet and adjust it for Par Fore league members to sign up for the tournament. Delete Instructions 2, 3, and 4 and replace them with a new Instruction 2: **Make check payable to P.F.G.L. and give to Lynn Doell, (513-555-6797)**. On the league sign-up sheet, make room for 30 members and 5 alternates.

### Job 48—Mailing to Golf Clubs

Prepare a letter of invitation to include with the sign-up sheets. This should be a form document to be merged with the data source listing the local golf clubs. A letter from a previous year's tournament is available, but it needs some repairs.
1. The Par Fore league is sponsoring this event.
2. The registration deadline is June 15, and the registration fee per golfer is $35. No refunds will be made after June 27.
3. Florence Rogers and Lynn Doell are co-chairpersons for the event. Be sure to include their phone numbers.
4. Check the letter carefully for further repairs and make it fit on one page.

*Job Narrative*

*Job 49—Handicap Conversion Chart*

Since the tournament requirement states that only 90 percent of the handicap will be used, it is sometimes handy to have a chart to make the conversions. Create a chart that lists handicaps from 1 to 36 and lists the 90 percent conversion. You may choose to have two or three double columns of numbers so the chart remains on one page. Make the chart attractive and easy to read.

*Job 50—Payroll Sheet & Job 51—Inventory*

Complete the payroll sheet for the fourth week in May. Fill in and calculate the inventory for the fourth Friday in May.

# JUNE

*Job 52—Weekly Sign-ups*

Prepare the weekly tournament sign-up sheets for June.

*Job 53—Petty Cash*

Since you worked with petty cash in April, the fund has been restored to the full $500. However, it recently was used for several items. Please complete the petty cash form so those items will be posted to the proper accounts. Janie Hodges made the purchases for the Pro Shop this time.

*Job 54—Slow Play*

Quite a number of members at the Ohio River Golf Club have been complaining about getting behind players who play slowly. In fact, slow play has begun to be a problem on the course. In discussing the problem, one of the golf pros mentioned that he worked at a course where "rangers" kept an eye on players and showed them ways to move more efficiently around the course. He got a copy of the information about rangering and began marking it up for corrections.

Jason has asked you to make those corrections and any others that need to be made in the document so the Ohio River association board can decide how they will implement this plan. Put the first page of the completed document on Ohio River letterhead. Make the document fit on two pages.

*Job 55—Checklist for Tournament*

Lynn and Florence have been concerned that they wouldn't get everything done for the invitational tournament by the time the tournament begins. So they created a checklist where each of them can initial an activity after the activity has been taken care of. They have asked you to make the checklist attractive for them and save it so it can be used for future tournaments.

*Job 56—Letter to Tournament Sponsors*

Each year the tournament chairmen request the sponsorship of the hole-in-one event. Local car dealerships are asked to donate a car as the prize for the first person in the invitational tournament to make a hole-in-one on a specific Par 3 hole. Prepare a form document similar to the one in the source documents and use the names and addresses given there. Put the letters on Par Fore stationery to be sent by Lynn Doell, Co-Chairperson. List her phone number under her name.

### Job 57—Invitational Deadline Poster

Registrations for Par Fore members to participate in the Invitational Tournament have been slow coming in. Lots of members are interested, but they have procrastinated. Create a single-page "ATTENTION" poster for the bulletin board reminding them of the deadline. Include the reminder that when they sign up, they must submit checks for $35 and mark cart and luncheon preferences.

### Job 58—Details with Pro Shop Staff

The Pro Shop staff is usually very helpful in getting ready for a tournament, but a checklist is a good idea there, too.

### Job 59—Payroll Sheet & Job 60—Inventory

Prepare the weekly payroll sheet for the hourly employees for the second week of June. Prepare the inventory list for the second week of June.

### Job 61—Slow Play Letter

The professionals and the Ohio River Association Board liked the idea of having rangers on the course to monitor members for slow play. The document you prepared will be distributed to all members of the club, along with a letter explaining the policy. The letter will come from the Ohio River Association Board. A copy of a letter from another golf club is available, but it needs to be edited so it will include Ohio River information, isn't so wordy, and fits on one page of Ohio River letterhead paper. Steve Whitney will be the ranger at Ohio River Golf Club. The television station where the golfing tapes will be played is WPRK. Key and edit the letter and prepare a final copy.

### Job 62—Change to Member Account

Pauline Downey, Member #41492, has just requested that her membership be reactivated. She would like to change from single golf to a family membership with a six-month trail fee, and both she and her husband would like lockers. There is no change to her address. Her husband's name is Paul, and their children are Pat and Pam. She'd like the membership to be activated as of June 15 of the current year. Fill out a member change form for Pauline to sign. Be sure it fits on one page.

### Job 63—Notice

A large number of people have signed up for the tournament—and more are wanting to participate. Prepare the notice for the bulletin board to help facilitate the filling of the Par Fore teams for the tournament.

### Job 64—Tournament List

The names of the 90 golfers from the 12 other clubs have been received and the starting holes assigned. Lynn has given you two lists—the names of the Par Fore golfers and the names of the guests. Each list includes their handicaps, hole assignments, and food choices. You will need to calculate the 90% handicap for the Par Fore golfers.

Sort the list in each of the following ways. Print each list.
1. Alphabetically (**job64a**)
2. By club, with the names alphabetized within the club groups (**job64b**)
3. By hole assignment (**job64c**)
4. By food choice (**job64d**)

### *Job 65—Check Request*

On June 17, Sue Staude, chairperson for table decorations, reported that she has spent $43.50 for materials for the decorations. Please fill out a check request so she can be reimbursed for the expenses before the end of the month. Charge it to cost code #48114. Lynn Doell, invitational co-chair, will have to authorize the payment. You may fill out the form using the computer, or you may print a copy of the form and fill it out by hand.

### *Job 66—Order Favors and Prizes*

Scott and Jason have been looking over the checklist for the invitational tournament and have realized that they need to order the favors and prizes immediately. Using the information from the Pro Shop Checklist, prepare an order form or letter ordering mugs, logo balls, tees and ball markers from: Golf 'n Stuff at 5650 Kenwood Road, Cincinnati, OH 45227, (513) 555-5060. Remember to add $5 for handling and shipping and 5% tax. It is already the third Monday of June, and you need these items no later than the fourth Tuesday. Your account number with this company is 9411-OR.

### *Job 67—List for Bulletin Board*

Prepare a one-page bulletin board announcement on Par Fore letterhead listing the members of the Par Fore league who will be participating in the invitational tournament. You may arrange the names in columns to make the text fit on one page. Double space the list of members and arrange them in alphabetic order so they can find their names easily.

### *Job 68—Function Sheet*

Complete the function sheet for the Invitational Tournament. The co-chairpersons are the contacts. Florence is to receive the billing. Include coffee/tea ($100) from 8 to 9 a.m., lunch from 1 p.m. to 3 p.m., and snack at the turn ($120), consisting of fruit and soft drinks. The Ohio River Dining Room is to be set up with round tables, and the color theme will be red, white, and blue. Request a registration table. The Par Fore committee will provide centerpieces for the tables. Be sure to include how many people signed up for each of the luncheon choices, which will be billed at $8.50 each. Keep the form on one page.

### *Job 69—Tournament Information*

A sheet detailing tournament rules and explaining the special events needs to be prepared. Each foursome will take a copy along on the course. Use Par Fore stationery, make any needed corrections, and make the information fit on one page. Make it attractive.

*Job 70—Reimbursement Request*

Jason Jarosik has given some additional lessons and repaired more clubs during his non-working hours. Member #23114 has had two more lessons, and Member #14782 had one lesson. Jason has repaired 3 clubs each for Members #17623 and #13456.

*Job 71—Hole-in-One*

On June (last Tuesday), Gordon Becker shot a hole-in-one on Hole 16 using a 3 iron. This accomplishment was witnessed by his partner, Dave Brantley, as well as Jane Trowbridge and Dorle Whitcomb. Hole 16 is 195 yards.

*Job 72—Volunteer Sign-up Sheet*

A sheet is needed for the bulletin board where league members can sign up to help with various tournament activities. Those activities and the number of people needed for each are listed on the checklist of tournament responsibilities. Use Par Fore stationery, and prepare a sign-up sheet with lines for the appropriate number of volunteers for each activity. Have the volunteers include their phone numbers.

*Job 73—Payroll Sheet & Job 74—Inventory*

Everyone has been working many hours to get ready for the Par Fore tournament. Prepare the payroll sheet for the fourth week of June so workers can be reimbursed for their efforts.

Prepare the inventory sheet for the fourth week of June.

# JULY

*Job 75—Weekly Sign-ups*

Prepare the weekly sign-up sheets for July. Also, some of the league members have been pestering you about wanting to sign up for events for the remainder of league play. Some will be out of town when the lists are posted, and the league board has ruled that it would be OK to post the weekly tournaments for the rest of the season.

Prepare the August sign-up sheets (save them as **job75b**) and September (save them as **job75c**).

*Job 76—Name Badges*

While name badges aren't necessary for the golfing part of the tournament, they are very desirable for the luncheon. Customize your **badge** form so it includes the first and last name of the player, followed by the club name. If necessary, convert your list of 120 tournament participants so it is a data source that can be merged with the revised **badge** form. When you finish with the merge, save the entire set of badges and print the first page only.

*Job 77—Signs*

The committee for the invitational has come to you with a couple of last-minute requests. They need signs for the tournament. You decide that standard 8½- by 11-inch paper used landscape will be fine. They have asked you to design a border for the signs to make them more attractive. You may use graphics borders, if your software has some.

### *Job 78—Pin Placement Sheet*

When guests play on an unfamiliar golf course, a pin placement sheet is helpful. The sheet provides information about each of the holes on the course. The sheet currently in use at Ohio River is handwritten. You have offered to make a more official-looking sheet using your word processing software.

### *Job 79—Winners' List*

The golfing for the tournament is over! It was a huge success, and the scores have been tallied. Use Par Fore letterhead to list the prize winners, their prizes, their clubs, and their scores.

### *Job 80—Certificates for Winners*

Each tournament winner is to receive a certificate recognizing his or her accomplishment. Prepare the 37 certificates. A keyboard merge would probably be the easiest way to set up this job (save the form file as **certificate**). Use a fancy page border or some kind of meaningful art on the certificate, and dress it up with fancy fonts so it looks official.

### *Job 81—Board Meeting Agenda*

Par Fore President Barb Krull has scheduled a board meeting for the Tuesday following the invitational tournament. Prepare an agenda using the same format you used in Job 41.

### *Job 82—Tournament Accounting*

All of the bills for the invitational tournament have been submitted for payment, and the tournament chairpersons have given you a list of the monies received and the monies spent. Prepare an income statement (using your software's template if possible), so they can present this at the board meeting. Print the statement on Par Fore stationery and make it look professional.

### *Job 83—Minutes of Board Meeting*

Don Ihlenfeld, league secretary, has given you a rough draft copy of the minutes of the recent board meeting. Prepare the minutes using the same format you used in Job 45.

### *Job 84—Payroll Sheet & Job 85—Inventory*

Complete the payroll sheet for the second week in July. Then fill out the inventory sheet for the second week in July.

*Job 86—Change to Member Account*

Alice Bricco, Member #31158, has requested that her membership be changed from family golf to single golf. She would like to begin using a locker at the clubhouse. These changes took place on July 14. Fill out the one-page member change form for Alice to sign.

*Job 87—Invitational Thank You Letters*

Invitational co-chairpersons Lynn Doell and Florence Rogers have asked you to send a merge letter to all of the people in the address book, thanking them for their time and effort in making the tournament such a success. Using Par Fore letterhead, acknowledge how each of them used his or her talents to make the tournament special to all who participated. Allow space for both Lynn and Florence to sign the letter. Save the form letter as **job87a**. Print the letters and envelopes. Do not save the merged letters.

Send a separate letter to Sue Staude, acknowledging her efforts in preparing the table decorations and asking her to personally thank each member of her committee. Save Sue's letter as **job87b**.

*Job 88—Hole-in-One*

Taisy Becker is celebrating her first hole-in-one. She used a 5 wood to drive 156 yards to a hole-in-one on the 11$^{th}$ hole during league play on the third week in July. Her partner, Betty Cartwright, Dorothy Charles, and Kay Ihlenfeld witnessed her accomplishment.

*Job 89—Payroll Sheet & Job 90—Inventory*

One of the other leagues at the Ohio River Golf Club has been preparing for a tournament, so all of the employees have more overtime hours. You're pleased to discover that many of the jobs you're being asked to complete are familiar to you because of the experience you had with the Par Fore Invitational. Prepare the payroll sheet for the fourth week in July.

Complete the inventory sheet for the fourth week of July.

---

Congratulations! You have now proven beyond a shadow of a doubt that you are a valued employee of the Ohio River Golf Club. If you completed all 90 of the jobs, you found that many of them were very easy. Some of them probably provided you with a challenge. The practice you received and the skills you acquired as you completed these jobs will be valuable to you as you use your word processing skills on the job.

# SOURCE DOCUMENTS

*Job 1*

(Suggested letterheads)

*Job 2* (the membership list)

Beatrice Cowling
3122 Barbara Lane
Cincinnati, OH 45244
513-555-8912

Carol Callahan
5392 Anchorage Road
Cincinnati, OH 45226
513-555-5035

Taisy Becker
46 Blue Boar Drive
Cincinnati, OH 45230
513-555-8922

Alice Bricco
14 Bridgeview Court
Cincinnati, OH 45248
513-555-6767

Gordon Becker
46 Blue Boar Drive
Cincinnati, OH 45230
513-555-8922

Beulah Seager
83A Arch Street
Cincinnati, OH 45202
513-555-8932

Dorothy Charles
12 Becky Court
Cincinnati, OH 45315
513-555-8942

Phoebe Phillips
132 Browning Street
Cincinnati, OH 45209
513-555-8952

Lucille Brennehan
793 Bett Lane
Cincinnati, OH 45238
513-555-8962

Jane Trowbridge
7833 Breezewood Drive
Cincinnati, OH 45248
513-555-8992

Kay Koclanes
113 Autumn Lane
Cincinnati, OH 45239
513-555-8902

Tim Koclanes
113 Autumn Lane
Cincinnati, OH 45239
513-555-8902

Alex Holbrook
3480 Bellmont
Cincinnati, OH 45227
513-555-6707

Christine Seitz
873B Boyde Street
Cincinnati, OH 45223
513-555-6717

Norm Seitz
873B Boyde Street
Cincinnati, OH 45223
513-555-6717

Sue Steiner
4513 Boggs Lane
Cincinnati, OH 45248
513-555-6727

Barb Krull
877 Bercliff Avenue, Apt. 34
Cincinnati, OH 45223
513-555-6737

Florence Rogers
88 Beach Hill
Cincinnati, OH 45223
513-555-6747

Leslie Rogers
88 Beach Hill
Cincinnati, OH 45223
513-555-6747

Margaret Dobbe
3349 Bevis Ave
Cincinnati, OH 45207
513-555-6757

Nancy Christianson
48 Brightview Drive
Cincinnati, OH 45231
513-555-6777

Sue Selle
4108 Bender Road
Cincinnati, OH 45233
513-555-6787

Eugene Selle
4108 Bender Road
Cincinnati, OH 45233
513-555-6787

Lynn Doell
1011 Ballard Street
Cincinnati, OH 45209
513-555-6797

Margot Babcock
1448 Bagdad Drive
Cincinnati, OH 45230
513-555-2401

Nancy Thiex
873 Beech Avenue
Cincinnati, OH 45205
513-555-2431

Warren Thiex
873 Beech Avenue
Cincinnati, OH 45205
513-555-2431

Sue Staude
1012 Baymiller Walk
Cincinnati, OH 45203
513-555-2441

Kay Ihlenfeld
862 Arnold Street
Cincinnati, OH 45208
513-555-2451

Don Ihlenfeld
862 Arnold Street
Cincinnati, OH 45208
513-555-2451

Theda Larsen
84 Biehl Street
Cincinnati, OH 45248
513-555-2481

Abe Larsen
84 Biehl Street
Cincinnati, OH 45248
513-555-2481

Gloria Arndt
4499 Andrew Street
Cincinnati, OH 45217
513-555-2491

Bob Arndt
4499 Andrew Street
Cincinnati, OH 45217
513-555-2491

Janine Anderson
71 Anders Court
Cincinnati, OH 45238
513-555-5015

Owen Anderson
71 Anders Court
Cincinnati, OH 45238
513-555-5015

Nancy Brantley
9130 Brantner Lane
Cincinnati, OH 45244
513-555-5025

Ted Forslin
Suite 46
14 Amor Place
Cincinnati, OH 45214
513-555-4296

Dave Brantley
9130 Brantner Lane
Cincinnati, OH 45244
513-555-5025

Dorle Whitcomb
872 Alphonse Lane
Cincinnati, OH 45238
513-555-5045

Ralph Harris
4201 Alexis Road
Cincinnati, OH 45239
513-555-5055

Betty Cartwright
48 Anna Mae Drive
Cincinnati, OH 45244
513-555-5075

Sue Jacobson
53 Airy Court
Cincinnati, OH 45239
513-555-5085

Peggy Eick
24 Ambrose Street
Cincinnati, OH 45224
513-555-5095

Gloria Staples
821 Alnetta Drive
Cincinnati, OH 45230
513-555-4286

Dennis Staples
821 Alnetta Drive
Cincinnati, OH 45230
513-555-4286

Emil Boneske
534 Alicemont Street
Cincinnati, OH 45209
513-555-4206

Jan Forslin
34 Amigo Court
Cincinnati, OH 45251
513-555-4216

Gail Larsen
3710 Aldrich Street
Cincinnati, OH 45231
513-555-4226

Judy Larsen
89 Alamosa Drive
Cincinnati, OH 45251
513-555-4236

Pauline Downey
43A Allenwood Ct.
Cincinnati, OH 45238
513-555-5065

Bonnie Larsen
Apartment 42
192 Allison Street
Cincinnati, OH 45212
513-555-4246

Sue Ihlenfeldt
32 Berman Meadow Drive
Cincinnati, OH 45243
513-555-4247

Ann Armstrong
51 Anniston Drive
Cincinnati, OH 45248
513-555-5005

*Job 3*

Dear (first name):

The 1997 Golf Season is just around the corner. The Bogey Buddies League will open the season with its annual Opening Day Luncheon on Tuesday, April 1, 1997, at noon at the Coachman's Inn Supper Club. Your newly elected officers will be introduced, and the head golf professional, Scott Alexejun, will welcome you with an update of golf-related developments including new USGA rules and additions to local rules at the Ohio River Golf Club. We will also preview the weekly events as well as local tournaments.

If you are planning on joining the Bogey Buddies Golf League, you will want to attend this Opening Luncheon. This is the time to renew friendships and meet new members. Please complete the form below and return it with your check by March 15 to the following address:

Ohio River Golf Club
Attention: Bogey Buddies Golf League
44 River Road
Cincinnati, OH 45227

As you know, the league is limited to 24 two-person teams, and the receipt of your check for dues will be processed on a first-come, first-in basis. Don't delay—insure your team's membership by sending in your dues today along with your reservation for the Opening Day Luncheon.

If you know of prospective members who might be interested in attending the luncheon, please call the pro shop and give us their names and numbers. We'll be happy to send out applications.

Good golfing,
The Golf Shop Staff

------------------------------------------

Name  _____
Address  _____
         _____

Phone Number: (Home) _____ (Work) _____
Team Member: _____
If you do not have a partner, do you want the pro shop staff to assign one?
          ____Yes ____ No
Dues: $25 for individual membership
Luncheon Cost: $10 per person (tax and gratuity included)

I _____will _____ will NOT be attending the Opening Day Luncheon.

                    Amount Enclosed: _____

**Job 4**

### PUEBLO PRODUCTS WEEKLY TIME SHEET

| Employee Name | | | | | Week Ending | |
|---|---|---|---|---|---|---|
| Employee Number | | | Department | | | |

| Day of Week | Morning | | Afternoon | | Daily Total | |
|---|---|---|---|---|---|---|
| | In | Out | In | Out | Reg Hrs | O/T Hrs |
| Wednesday | | | | | | |
| Thursday | | | | | | |
| Friday | | | | | | |
| Saturday | | | | | | |
| Sunday | | | | | | |
| Monday | | | | | | |
| Tuesday | | | | | | |
| Total | | | | | | |

| Overtime Authorized By | | Employee Signature | |
|---|---|---|---|
| Comments | | | |

**Job 5**

### PRO SHOP DAILY CLOSEOUT

Cash on hand per closeout $ _____

Total cash drawer $ _____

Less float $ _____

Total deposit $ _____ $ _____

Difference between deposit and closeout $ _____

Reason for difference _____

_____

_____

Closed by _____ Date _____

The end-of-day work must be balanced before forwarding to accounting. When the error is located, a copy of the ticket(s) that has caused the problem must be photocopied and placed for correction by accounting.

**Job 7**

NOTICE

TO ALL MEMBERS, GUESTS, AND EMPLOYEES:
PARKING IS NOT PERMITTED IN THE SERVICE AREA.
HANDICAP PARKING WITH PERMIT ONLY
THANK YOU!

*Source Documents*

## Job 8

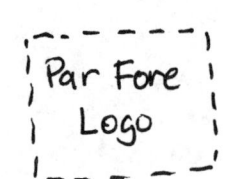

[Par Fore Logo]

**Par Fore Golf League**
**Weekly Special Event**
**Prize List**

Event _____

Date _____

| Team | Player | Place | Prize |
|------|--------|-------|-------|
|      |        |       |       |
|      |        |       |       |

## Job 9

### Ohio River Golf Club
**Payroll for Hourly Clubhouse Employees**

Pay Period Ending: KEYBOARD()

| Emp. No. | Employee | Rate | Regular Hours | Overtime @ 1½ Regular | Total Hours | Total Pay |
|----------|----------|------|---------------|----------------------|-------------|-----------|
| 149 | Barbara Telander | $12.75 | KEYBOARD() | KEYBOARD() | 0 | $0.00 |
| 233 | Janie Hodges | $9.25 | KEYBOARD() | KEYBOARD() | 0 | $0.00 |
| 218 | Gene Shultz | $10.00 | KEYBOARD() | KEYBOARD() | 0 | $0.00 |
| 309 | (Your name) | $8.50 | KEYBOARD() | KEYBOARD() | 0 | $0.00 |

## Job 10

Barbara Telander    Regular Hours – 35, Overtime – 0
Janie Hodges        Regular Hours – 35, Overtime – 0
Gene Shultz         Regular Hours – 35, Overtime – 1
(Your name)         Regular Hours – 35, Overtime – 0

## Job 11

Scott Alexejun
1432 Boggs Lane
Cincinnati, OH 45246
513-555-9422

Barbara Telander
4399 Baymiller Walk
Cincinnati, OH 45203
513-555-8933

Gene Shultz
552 Belsaw Place
Cincinnati, OH 45220
513-555-8944

Jason Jarosik
42 Bear Valley Court
Cincinnati, OH 45241
513-555-8991

Janie Hodges
13D Boyde Street
Cincinnati, OH 45223
513-555-6772

(Add your name and address.)

Job 12

# Hole-in-One

Name:        (Player)
Date:        (Date of Hole-in-One)
Hole:        (Hole where play was made)
Yardage:     (Length of the hole)
Club Used:   (Club)
Witnesses:   (Players who witnessed the event)
Checklist:

_____ Copy of Scorecard
_____ Give player Golf Digest form
_____ Order plaque for player (Insta-Plak #35 — Call 888-555-3411 and charge code 1029)
_____ Report to USGA (800-555-7816)
_____ Copy for newsletter and local radio stations (6)
_____ Letter from Professional
_____ Send wall engraving to Happy Golfers, 513-555-0443

Miscellaneous Notes:

_____
_____
_____

# Ohio River Golf Club

## Function Sheet

| Date of Event | Day of the Week | Booked |
|---|---|---|
|  |  |  |

| Contact #1 | Work Phone | Fax |
|---|---|---|
|  |  |  |

| Contact #2 | Work Phone | Fax |
|---|---|---|
|  |  |  |

| Group Name | Number of Guests |
|---|---|
|  |  |

| Billing Name and Address | Cost |
|---|---|
|  |  |

| Type of Function | Meeting Room | Break-out Room |
|---|---|---|
|  |  |  |

| Break | Room Arrangement | Audio Visual |
|---|---|---|
| Begin<br>End | □ Classroom<br>□ Theater<br>□ U-Shape<br>□ T-Shape<br>□ Rounds<br>□ Display Table<br>□ Registration Table<br>□ Break Table<br>□ Speaker's Table<br>□ Material Table<br>□ Conference Table<br>□ Other | □ Flip Chart<br>□ Overhead<br>□ Screen<br>□ TV and VCR<br>□ Slide Projector<br>□ Extension Cords<br>□ Podium<br>□ Microphone<br>□ Other |
| **Luncheon** | | |
| Begin<br>End | | |
| **Dinner** | | |
| Begin<br>End | | |

| Menu (With Pricing) | Colors/Centerpieces |
|---|---|
|  |  |

A guarantee of attendance for all food events will be required 48 hours in advance. The Club will prepare and set for 5% over guaranteed attendance. All food and beverage items are subject to 16% service charge and a 5% sales tax. All charges are subject to a 1.5% monthly finance fee after thirty days. Cancellation of this event within 5 calendar days of the scheduled date will result in the assessment equal to 90% of all ordered services or products.

| Signature of Customer/Date | Ohio River Golf Club Representative/Date |
|---|---|

44 River Road
Cincinnati, Ohio 45227
513-555-GOLF (4653)

*Job 14*

```
         CART MAINTENANCE
           REPAIR ORDER

Cart # _____  Model # _____  Date: _____
Cart Make:
        _____ Club Car
        _____ E-Z Go
        _____ Yahmaha
        _____ Other: _____
Problem: _____
_____
_____
Repair Needed: _____
_____
Parts Needed: _____
_____

Work Completed by: _____
Date: _____
```

*Job 15*

| | |
|---|---|
| Barbara Telander | Regular Hours - 35, Overtime Hours - 0 |
| Janie Hodges | Reg - 35, Over - 0 |
| Gene Shultz | Reg - 35, Over - 1 |
| (Your name) | Reg - 35, Over - 0 |

*Job 16*

```
                    CHECK REQUEST
    (TO BE USED WHEN REQUESTING CHECKS WITHOUT AN INVOICE OR RECEIPT)

PLEASE ISSUE A CHECK IN THE AMOUNT OF $ _____

FOR _____

PAYABLE TO _____

ADDRESS _____

TO BE CHARGED TO _____
                        (COST CODE)

DATE REQUIRED _____

REQUESTED BY _____ DATE _____

AUTHORIZED BY _____
```

*Job 17*

RULES OF PLAY

USGA RULES WILL GOVERN ALL PLAY EXCEPT AS MODIFIED BY LOCAL RULES
*PLEASE READ AND REFER OFTEN TO YOUR COPY OF THE USGA RULE BOOK*

<u>EMBEDDED</u> <u>BALL</u> rule will be in effect through the green. (USGA RULE 25.2)

<u>WASTE</u> <u>AREAS</u>: All sand areas with grass or bushes shall be played as rough, i.e., you may take a practice swing, ground your club and remove loose impediments.

<u>RELIEF</u> from the following obstacles entitles you to a free drop. (PROCEDURE USGA RULE 13).

**Source Documents**

OBSTRUCTIONS—IMMOVABLE (USGA RULE 24.2) Interference occurs when a ball lies in or on the obstruction, or so close that the obstruction interferes with the player's STANCE or the area of his NATURAL INTENDED SWING.
- Artificially surfaced cart paths, paved or freshly pine needled.
- Worn extensions of cart paths.
- Sprinkler control boxes.
- Newly planted trees, mounded or staked.

ABNORMAL GROUND CONDITIONS (USGA RULE 25)
- GUR—ground under repair is any portion of the course so marked or declared by the proshop.
- CASUAL WATER—any temporary accumulation of water visible before or after player takes his stance.
- HOLE CAST OR RUNWAY made by a burrowing animal, reptile or bird.

HAZARDS— Marked by yellow lines or stakes (WATER HAZARD)
Marked by red lines or stakes (LATERAL WATER HAZARD)
NOTE: Lines always take precedence over stakes as margin of the hazard.

OUT OF BOUNDS—White stakes marking out of bounds or any boundary defining golf course property such as roads and fences. NOTE: OB markers are not considered obstructions and may NOT be removed and DO NOT entitle player to a free drop.

FREE DROP—With no penalty you may, after taking your natural stance, drop the ball one club length from your stance, but no nearer to the hole.

PROVISIONAL BALL—PROCEDURE, USGA RULE 27-2.

PENALTIES— *Ball in Water Hazard*, (USGA RULE 26) - *Ball lost or out of bounds*, (USGA RULE 27) - *Unplayable*, (USGA RULE 28).

*Job 19*

### Ohio River Golf Club Pro Shop
#### Standard Merchandise
#### Weekly Sales Report
Week Ending _____

$H = (E * C) * .05$

$F = (E - D) / D$

$G = (E - D) * C$

| Stock Code | Description | Qty. Sold | Wholesale Price | Retail Price | % Markup | Net Income | Tax Generated at 5% |
|---|---|---|---|---|---|---|---|
| A | B | C | D | E | F | G | H |

| Code | Description | Wholesale | Retail |
|---|---|---|---|
| 1027 | Club Rentals | 35.00 | 35.00 |
| 1028 | Club Repair | 5.00 | 5.00 |
| 1001 | Men's Shirts | 25.00 | 42.00 |
| 1002 | Men's Shorts | 28.00 | 48.00 |
| 1003 | Men's Sweaters | 39.00 | 66.00 |
| 1004 | Men's Slacks | 37.00 | 55.00 |
| 1005 | Ladies' Shirts | 24.00 | 42.00 |
| 1006 | Ladies' Shorts | 27.00 | 48.00 |
| 1007 | Ladies' Sweaters | 39.00 | 60.00 |
| 1009 | Windshirts | 35.00 | 52.00 |
| 1010 | Sweatshirts | 25.00 | 39.00 |
| 1011 | Accessories | 10.00 | 15.00 |
| 1012 | Glasses | 3.00 | 10.00 |
| 1013 | Umbrella | 12.00 | 20.00 |

Quantities sold during the second week in March:

| Item | Quantity | Item | Quantity |
|---|---|---|---|
| 1027 | 2 | 1011 | 7 |
| 1028 | 2 | 1012 | 6 |
| 1001 | 6 | 1015 | 4 |
| 1002 | 1 | 1016 | 1 |
| 1005 | 4 | 1020 | 3 |
| 1006 | 2 | 1050 | 1 |
|  |  | 1061 | 1 |

| | | | |
|---|---|---|---|
| 1014 | Headcovers | 7.00 | 15.00 |
| 1015 | Shoes | 60.00 | 85.00 |
| 1016 | Golf Gloves | 8.00 | 12.00 |
| 1017 | Logo Balls | 1.00 | 2.50 |
| 1020 | Headwear | 6.00 | 12.00 |
| 1021 | Steel Shafted Irons | 40.00 | 45.00 |
| 1022 | Graphite Irons | 70.00 | 78.00 |
| 1023 | Titanium Head Irons | 85.00 | 98.00 |
| 1024 | Graphite Woods | 175.00 | 220.00 |
| 1025 | Titanium Woods | 220.00 | 289.00 |
| 1026 | Miscellaneous Clubs | 70.00 | 85.00 |
| 1049 | Golf Bags | 135.00 | 160.00 |
| 1050 | Putters | 75.00 | 90.00 |
| 1054 | Soft Spikes | 4.00 | 5.00 |
| 1061 | USGA Rule Book | 10.00 | 12.00 |

## Job 20

*Barbara Telander* — Regular Hours - 37, Overtime Hours - 0
*Janie Hodges* — Regular Hours - 37, Overtime Hours - 1
*Gene Shultz* — Regular Hours - 37, Overtime Hours - 0
*(Your name)* — Regular Hours - 37, Overtime Hours - 0

## Job 21

### BOGEY BUDDIES GOLF LEAGUE
### BYLAWS

#### ARTICLE I - NAME AND DEFINITION

The name of this organization shall be the Ohio River Bogey Buddies Golf League. The organization shall be comprised of members of the Ohio River Golf Club. Any member who has an Ohio River Golf Club USGA handicap of 40 or lower is elligible to join for the season.

#### ARTICLE II - PURPOSE

The purpose of the Bogey Buddies league shall be to promote sociability and interest in the game of golf among the members of Bogey Buddies and to regulate and govern all contests among its members.

#### ARTICLE III - SEASON

The regular season shall begin on or about April 1 and close on or about October 1.

#### ARTICLE IV - MEMBERSHIP

1. Upon payment of annual dues, to be determined by the Executive Board, members may participate in events scheduled by the Bogey Buddies during the course of the season. Dues will cover April through September and will not be pro-rated.

2. Each member shall agree to comply with and be bound by the bylaws, rules and regulations of the league.

3. Transferred handicap cards from other USGA courses are acceptable. However, they must show the last twenty scores, course rating and slope. This information will be used by the Handicap

Chairman to calculate an Ohio River Golf Club handicap. This handicap may be used in competition. The scores from the member's card must be entered into the computer, by the proshop, as "away" scores with the applicable rating and slope. A new member without a valid USGA handicap card must return five (5) scorecards from Ohio River Golf Club, thus establishing an Ohio River Golf Club handicap. If neither of the above is available, the applicant may play in Bogey Buddies events but not in competition.

## ARTICLE V - EXECUTIVE BOARD

The Executive Board shall be composed of the elected officers of the league, i.e., the President, Vice President, Secretary and Treasurer, and also the Tournament Chairman, Handicap Chairman and Membership Chairman. The imediate past President shall sit on the Board in an advisory capacity.

1. The President shall preside at all meetings of the league and of the Executive Board. The President shall select chairmen of all standing and special committees and shall be an ex-officio member of all committees except the nominating commitee. The President shall appoint a committee to audit the financial records of the association on an annual basis and such committee shall give their report at the annual April meeting. The President, with the Executive Board, shall prepare a proposed budget for the year within six weeks after the opening date.

2. The Vice-President shall preside at meeting in the absence of the President and shall perform other duties as requested by the President. The Vice-President shall also assist the Tournament Chairman.

3. The Secretary shall keep all records of proceeding at all meetings and shall handle necessary correspondence.

4. The Treasurer shall keep a full and accurate account of all moneys. The Treasurer and the President shall have authority to sign all checks and deposit moneys. Two (2) signatures shall be required on each disbursed Bogey Buddies check.

## ARTICLE VI - ELECTIONS AND TERMS OF OFFICE

1. The Nominating Committee shall be composed of five (5) members: the Chairman, appointed by the President, three members who shall be nominated from the floor at the opening meeting, and one volunteer member from the Executive Board.

2. After the meeting of the committee, the Nominating Committee Chairman shall contact the nominees for President, Vice-President, Secretary, and Treasurer to ascertain their willingness to accept office. The sleate is reported to the Executive Board and then posted on the bulleting board two (2) weeks prior to the Fall Luncheon meeting.

3. Candidates other than those chosen by the Nominating Committee may be added to the slate if the candidate signifies to the committee his/her willingness to accept office. Names of such nominees must be posted at least seven (7) days prior to the election.

4. Prior to the meeting, an absentee ballot may be submitted to the Chairman of the Nominating Committee. It should be enclosed in an envelope bearing the signature of the member. Alternatively, a member may submit a proxy.

5. Elections shall be held at the Fall Luncheon meeting. Written ballots will be issued if there is a competition for any office. The majority vote shall be necessary for election. Installation will take place at the Closing Luncheon meeting where upon all the officers shall take office immediately. The term of office is one (1) year. No member shall hold the same office for more than two (2) consecutive terms.

6. In the event of a vacancy in any office, the Executive Board shall appoint a member to fill the office for the remainder of the term.

## ARTICLE VII - STANDING COMMITTEES

1. The standing committees of the league shall be:

   | | | |
   |---|---|---|
   | Tournament | Rules | Membership |
   | Hospitality | Publicity | Handicap |
   | Prize | Telephone | Sunshine |

   a. The Tournament commitee shall plan, provide rules and supervise all tournaments, league events and all special events. A schedule for the season shall be presented to the Executive Board for approval. Tournement descriptions as written in the handbook are not subject to change without approval of the Executive Board.

   b. The Rules committee shall promote knowledge of the rules of golf among the membership. They will familiarize themselves with the USGA rules of golf as well as all local rules.

   c. The Prize committee is responsible for selecting awards for the major tournaments. The chairman shall be responsible for the purchasing and engraving of existing and future plaques and trophies.

   d. The Hospitality committee shall be responsible for social arrangements for the General Meetings. The dates of all social activities for the season shall be given to the Club manager at least two (2) months prior to the season opening.

   e. The Publicity committee shall furnish information to the club newspaper and the press for all upcoming and past events of the association. Pictures shall be taken at all major functions and added to the current scrapbook.

   f. The Telephone committee shall contact the membership whenever the need arises.

   g. The Membership committee shall compile the annual handbook and roster of the league. The Chairman shall be responsible for the publication of the application for membership.

   h. The Handicap committee shall be responsible for all aspects of handicapping in accordance with the USGA.

   i. The Sunshine committee shall be responsible for sending get-well or sympathy cards to members who are ill or have a death in the family and for sending an appropriate gift in the case of death of a member or the spouse of a member.

2. Before the opening of the season, the Executive Board shall meet with the chairman of the standing committees to plan the schedule and to discuss any other pertinent business. Additional meetings of this group may be called as needed.

## ARTICLE VIII - MEETINGS

1. There shall be a minimum of three (3) General Meetings each year. These meetings shall be: Opening Day, Nominating Committee formed; Fall Luncheon, Election of Officers; Closing Luncheon, Installation of Officers.

2. Special meetings may be called by the President at any time or on written request of fifteen (15) members of the association addressed to the President.

3. All members of the league are eligible to vote in all regular and special meetings. This right extends to all officers except the President, who may vote only in the event of a tie.

4. A quorum for a meeting of the league to conduct business or elections shall be fifty percent (50%) of the members.

*Source Documents*

## ARTICLE IX - AMENDMENTS

These Bylaws may be amended at any meeting by two-thirds (2/3) of the votes cast, provided that the number voting constitutes a quorum. Proposed amendment(s) shall have been prominently posted for at least ten (10) days prior to the meeting at which the amendment(s) is to be acted upon.

## ARTICLE X - PARLIAMENTARY AUTHORITY

The rules contained in the current edition of ROBERT'S RULES OF ORDER NEWLY REVISED shall govern the association in all cases to which they are applicable and in which they are consistant with these Bylaws and any special rules of order the league may adopt.

REVISED (insert current date)

## *Job 22*

### DESCRIPTIONS OF LEAGUE EVENTS

**ALTERNATE SHOT:** 2-Player teams flighted according to team handicap. Each player tees off on all holes and each hits the other's second shot. After the second shot, team selects the best shot and then alternates shots until the ball is holed out. Repeat this procedure from each tee.

**BEST BALL FORMAT:** Best net ball per hole.

**LOW GROSS/NET:** Team members are flighted on individual handycap using full handicap in net division.

**NASSAU:** Play 18 holes, post gross and net scores. No duplicate winners (can win only once). Low Gross overall, Low Net overall, Low Gross front nine, Low Gross back nine, Low Net front nine, Low Net back nine.

**ODD/EVEN:** Two-player teams. One player's score used on odd holes and the other players score used on the even holes.

**SCRAMBLE:** Each player tees off and best shot is selected. All team members than play from that spot no nearer to the hole. Follow this procedure throughout the round.

**TOTAL NET:** Total net score of foursome combined.

**QUOTA POINTS:** Gross score. Points: 1 for bogy; 2 for par; 4 for birdie; 8 for eagle; and 10 for hole in one. Your first quota will be the difference between 36 and your handicap. In subsequent games, your quota will increase by one point for each 3 points by which you exceed your quota or will decrease by 1 point for each 3 points below your quota. These updated quotas will be used each time a quota game is played.

**WEEKLY SKINS:** Skins game (flighted). Optional $2 to pro shop if you wish to participate.

## *Job 23*

### PLAYER'S RESPONSIBILITIES & TOURNAMENT POLICIES

1. In order to participate in any tournament (weekly or major), a person must be a member of the Bogey Buddies Golf League. If not participating, you cannot follow the field, and guests are not allowed.

2. Entrants for all events must sign up in advance. Sign-up sheets will be posted in the pro shop. Tee times are posted on the bulletin board outside the pro shop. PLEASE call the pro shop if you want to cancel.

3. New members must establish an Ohio River Golf Club handicap, or transfer from another club a current USGA handicap card for 18 holes not to exceed 40.

4. All play shall be goverened by USGA Rules of Golf and local rules. (See RULES OF PLAY)

5. On league day, the ball must be played through the hole, EXCEPT when the hole is not counted in the particalar tournament.

6. Check score cards for accuracy prior to attesting, signing, and dating. There will be a player disqualification for unsigned or incorrect cards.

7. Actual number scored on hole is to be posted on card, and adjustment is to be made using the equitable stroke control procedure before computer entry. See "Adjusting Scores" bulleting posted in the locker rooms.

8. Leave an attested, signed, and dated score card in the Weekly Tournament Box in the pro shop.

9. Consistent with the USGA Rules of Golf, any delay, suspension, or cancelation of play because of weather or course conditions will be made by the Tournament Chairman in accordance with the golf professional's advice. Rescheduling events will be done by the Tournament Chairman, if necessary.

10. The membership will be notified three (3) weeks in advance of any tournament changes.

11. Any questions regarding rules should be directed to the Rules Chairman.

12. Courtesy and consideration for other players on the coarse requires that no one should move, talk, or stand too close or directly behind the ball or the hole when a player is addressing the ball or making a stroke.

13. Slow play should be avoided by going to your ball whenever possible and being ready to hit; sizing up your shot and deciding which club you will use while others are hitting; not taking unnecessary practice swings; not over-reading the putting greens; moving away from greens to next tee as soon as possible before entering scores on card.

14. All players are expected and required to wear proper atire at all times. Dresses, skirts, slacks, golf shorts up to four inches above the knee, and golf shirts are considered appropriate attire. Halter tops, tee shirts, bathing suits, sweat pants, jeans, tennis attire or athletic shorts more than four inches above the knee are not permitted.

*Job 24* (the schedule)

(Year) WEEKLY TOURNAMENT SCHEDULE

| APRIL | First Week | OPENING LUNCHEON AND SCRAMBLE |
| | Second Week | Best Ball |
| | Third Week | Quota Points |
| | Fourth Week | Alternate Shot |

| | | |
|---|---|---|
| MAY | First Week | Odd/Even |
| | Second Week | Total Net |
| | Third Week | Quota Points |
| | Fourth Week | Low Gross/Net |
| JUNE | First Week | Nassau |
| | Second Week | Scramble |
| | Third Week | Best Ball |
| | Fourth Week | Quota Points |
| JULY | First Week | INVITATIONAL TOURNAMENT |
| | Second Week | Total Net |
| | Third Week | Quota Points |
| | Fourth Week | Alternate Shot |
| AUGUST | First Week | Scramble |
| | Second Week | Best Ball |
| | Third Week | Odd/Even |
| | Fourth Week | Quota Points |
| SEPTEMBER | First Week | Nassau |
| | Second Week | Low Gross/Net |
| | Third Week | Quota Points |
| | Fourth Week | CLOSING LUNCHEON AND SCRAMBLE |

*Job 24* (the sign-up sheet)

**WEEKLY TOURNAMENT
SIGN-UP SHEET**

Date:
Tournament Format:

Sign up for the Weekly Tournament in the list below. Be sure to put BOTH team members' names in box. Good Luck!

| 1. | 9. | 17. |
|---|---|---|
| | | |
| 2. | 10. | 18. |
| | | |
| 3. | 11. | 19. |
| | | |
| 4. | 12. | 20. |
| | | |

| 5. | 13. | 21. |
|---|---|---|
| 6. | 14. | 22. |
| 7. | 15. | 23. |
| 8. | 16. | 24. |

## Job 25

Ann Armstrong
Carol Callahan
Pauline Downey
Alice Bricco

**Members to Delete**

Lillian Mitchell
4552 Blue Spruce Road
Cincinnati, OH 45223
513-555-8972

Louis Mitchell
4552 Blue Spruce Road
Cincinnati, OH 45223
513-555-8972

Jean Van Alsteen
Apt. 17C
78 Budmar Street
Cincinnati, OH 45224
513-555-8982

John Van Alsteen
Apt. 17C
78 Budmar Street
Cincinnati, OH 45224
513-555-8982

**Members to Add**

## Job 26

| Barbara | Reg - 37, Overtime - 1 |
| Janie | Reg - 37, Overtime - 0 |
| Gene | Reg - 37, Overtime - 0 |
| (Yours) | Reg - 37, Overtime - 4 |

## Job 27

Quantities sold during the fourth week in March:

| Item | Quan | Item | Quan |
|---|---|---|---|
| 1027 | 3 | 1012 | 2 |
| 1001 | 3 | 1014 | 1 |
| 1003 | 2 | 1022 | 1 |
| 1007 | 1 | | |

*Job 28*

## Ohio River Golf Club
### Where Great Golf Never Ends

- Lessons by PGA Professionals
- Golf Range
- Club repair, refinishing, & regripping
- Annual hole-in-one club

- Pro Shop with all equipment you need
- Custom club fitting
- Bags and accessories
- Carts
- Clothing

513-555-GOLF (4653)
44 River Road, Cincinnati

Open 7 days a week, 7 am until dark

---

*Job 29*

Par Fore League, (Year) Team Assignments

| | | | | | |
|---|---|---|---|---|---|
| Team 1 | Christine Seitz<br>Eugene Selle | Team 10 | Kay Koclanes<br>Beulah Seager | Team 19 | Gordon Becker<br>Dave Brantley |
| Team 2 | Norm Seitz<br>Sue Selle | Team 11 | Tim Koclanes<br>Abe Larsen | Team 20 | Dorothy Charles<br>Kay Ihlenfeld |
| Team 3 | Gloria Staples<br>Nancy Thiex | Team 12 | Warren Thiex<br>John Van Alsteen | Team 21 | Alex Holbrook<br>Ted Forslin |
| Team 4 | Ralph Harris<br>Don Ihlenfeld | Team 13 | Dennis Staples<br>Jean Van Alsteen | Team 22 | Sue Steiner<br>Lynn Doell |
| Team 5 | Sue Jacobson<br>Barb Krull | Team 14 | Margaret Dobbe<br>Phoebe Phillips | Team 23 | Theda Larsen<br>Florence Rogers |
| Team 6 | Janine Anderson<br>Bob Arndt | Team 15 | Beatrice Cowling<br>Lucille Brennehan | Team 24 | Sue Staude<br>Leslie Rogers |
| Team 7 | Owen Anderson<br>Gloria Arndt | Team 16 | Margot Babcock<br>Nancy Christianson | Alternates: | Emil Boneske<br>Jan Forslin<br>Sue Ihlenfeldt<br>Bonnie Larsen<br>Gail Larsen<br>Judy Larsen |
| Team 8 | Jane Trowbridge<br>Dorle Whitcomb | Team 17 | Betty Cartwright<br>Taisy Becker | | |
| Team 9 | Lillian Mitchell<br>Louis Mitchell | Team 18 | Nancy Brantley<br>Peggy Eick | | |

**Job 29** (continued)

### Par Fore League
### Opening Day Luncheon

| Member Name | Team Number | Phone | Luncheon Paid (date received) | Attended Luncheon | Materials Received |
|---|---|---|---|---|---|
| A | | | | | |
| Janine Anderson | 6 | 513-555-5015 | | | |

**Job 31**

#### SEVEN HILLS
#### REQUEST FOR REIMBURSEMENT

The following is to be added to my paycheck for reimbursement of
Lessons charged to account of _____ $ _____
_____ $ _____
_____ $ _____
_____ $ _____
_____ $ _____

Total due for lessons $ _____
Club repairs charged to _____ $ _____
_____ $ _____
_____ $ _____
_____ $ _____

Total due for club repairs $ _____
Total of this request $ _____

Requested by _____ Date _____

**Job 32**

| | |
|---|---|
| Barbara | Reg – 40, Overtime – 2 |
| Janie | Reg – 40, Overtime – 1 |
| Gene | Reg – 40, Overtime – 4 |
| (Yours) | Reg – 40, Overtime – 2 |

New Employee: #449 – Jack Schwab
@ $7.00 per hour – 24 Hours (regular)

**Job 33**

Quantities sold during the second week in April:

| Item | Quan | Item | Quan |
|---|---|---|---|
| 1027 | 1 | 1016 | 2 |
| 1002 | 2 | 1017 | 4 |
| 1005 | 3 | 1026 | 2 |
| 1007 | 3 | 1046 | 1 |
| 1009 | 2 | 1050 | 1 |
| 1011 | 2 | 1061 | 3 |
| 1013 | 1 | | |

**Job 34**

| Cost Code | Recipient | Item | Amount |
|---|---|---|---|
| | | | |
| | | Total This Check Request | |
| | | Original Petty Cash Balance | $500.00 |
| | | Balance in Petty Cash | |

Job 35

| Member Name | | Member # | Effective Date |
|---|---|---|---|
| Add Trail Fee | ☐ Full Year<br>☐ Six Months | | |
| Delete Trail Fee | ☐ | | |
| Delete Cart Lease | ☐ | | |
| Add Monthly Locker Fee | | ☐ Men<br>☐ Women | |
| Delete Locker Fee ☐<br>(Turned in Key)<br>☐ Yes ☐ No | | ☐ Men<br>☐ Women | |
| Change Address | | ☐ Permanent<br>☐ Temporary | |

| | | | |
|---|---|---|---|
| Activate Membership ☐ | | | |
| Cancel Membership ☐ | | | |
| Change Membership From ☐ Single Golf<br>To ☐ Single Golf | | ☐ Family Golf<br>☐ Family Golf | ☐ Social<br>☐ Social |
| Other Changes (please specify) | | | |

_____    _____    _____
(Member signature)     (date)     (staff signature)

Job 36

Code 3349, Telephone Note Pads, 10 @ $2.95 each
Code 3349, Pens for Pro Shop use, package of 12 for $3.95
Code 4427, Pencils for Keeping Scores, 4 dozen @ $3.76 per dozen

## Job 37

Black Diamond Country Club
3333 West Black Diamond Circle
Forest Park, OH 45240
(513) 555-3446

Delhi Hills Country Club
8161 Hampton Street
Delhi Hills, OH 45238
(513) 555-8161

Brooksville Golf & Country Club
23446 Links Drive
Deer Park, OH 45236
(513) 555-8879

Oak Hills Country Club
10059 Northcliffe Blvd.
Cherry Grove, OH 45230
(513) 555-6830

Seven Rivers Golf & Country Club
P.O. Box 1146
Blue Ash, OH 45242
(513) 555-7712

Silver Springs Golf & Country Club
3535 Trophy Blvd.
Covington, KY 41011
(410) 555-0021

River View Golf Club
12 River Road
Cincinnati, OH 45227
(513) 555-8711

Chaska Country Club
4400 Oak Drive
White Oak, OH 45154
(513) 555-4230

Sharon Woods Golf Club
13140 East Cornell Road
Brecon, OH 45242
(513) 555-7771

Seven Hills Country Club
55821 Springdale Road
Seven Hills, OH 45231
(513) 555-8822

Seville Golf & Country Club
42 Clocktower Parkway
Norwood, OH 45212
(513) 555-2276

Glenview Golf Club
22 Winton Woods Court
Greenhills, OH 45218
(513) 555-9012

## Job 38

| | |
|---|---|
| Barbara | Reg - 40, Overtime - 1 |
| Janie | Reg - 40, Overtime - 1-1/2 |
| Gene | Reg - 40, Overtime - 2 |
| (Yours) | Reg - 40, Overtime - 1 |
| Jack | Reg - 22 |

## Job 39

Quantities sold during the fourth week in April:

| Item | Quan | Item | Quan |
|---|---|---|---|
| 1027 | 4 | 1014 | 3 |
| 1028 | 1 | 1015 | 1 |
| 1001 | 1 | 1016 | 1 |
| 1002 | 1 | 1017 | 3 |
| 1005 | 2 | 1020 | 2 |
| 1006 | 1 | 1021 | 2 |
| 1010 | 1 | 1026 | 1 |
| 1012 | 2 | 1061 | 1 |
| 1013 | 1 | | |

*Job 41*

AGENDA
PAR FORE BOARD MEETING
MAY (first Tuesday), (year)
1:00 pm Club Room

CALL TO ORDER . . . . . . . . . . . . . . . . . . . . . . . . . . . . . . . . . . . . . . . . . . . . . . . . . . . . . . . . . . . . . . (President)
READING OF MINUTES . . . . . . . . . . . . . . . . . . . . . . . . . . . . . . . . . . . . . . . . . . . . . . . . . . . . . . . . (Secretary)
TREASURER'S REPORT . . . . . . . . . . . . . . . . . . . . . . . . . . . . . . . . . . . . . . . . . . . . . . . . . . . . . . . . (Treasurer)
COMMITTEE REPORTS:
    Membership . . . . . . . . . . . . . . . . . . . . . . . . . . . . . . . . . . . . . . . . . . (Membership Chairperson)
    Rules . . . . . . . . . . . . . . . . . . . . . . . . . . . . . . . . . . . . . . . . . . . . . . . . . . . . . (Rules Chairperson)
    Handicap . . . . . . . . . . . . . . . . . . . . . . . . . . . . . . . . . . . . . . . . . . . . . . (Handicap Chairperson)
    Tournaments . . . . . . . . . . . . . . . . . . . . . . . . . . . . . . . . . . . . . . . . . (Tournament Chairperson)
        Invitational Tournament: . . . . . . . . . . . . . . . . . . . . . . . . . . . . . (Invitational Chairperson)
            Clubs Invited
            Tournament Format
            Prizes
            Meal Functions
            Miscellaneous Items
OLD BUSINESS . . . . . . . . . . . . . . . . . . . . . . . . . . . . . . . . . . . . . . . . . . . . . . . . . . . . . . . . . . . . . . . (President)
NEW BUSINESS . . . . . . . . . . . . . . . . . . . . . . . . . . . . . . . . . . . . . . . . . . . . . . . . . . . . . . . . . . . . . . (President)
ADJOURNMENT


*Job 42*

*BUDGET*
*for*
*(year) INVITATIONAL TOURNAMENT*

*Projected Expenses:*

| | | |
|---|---:|---:|
| Luncheon: 120 @ $12 | | $1,440.00 |
| Welcome Coffee | | 100.00 |
| Golf Cart fee for Guests 60 @ $5 | | 300.00 |
| Prize Fee (Pro Shop Certificates) | | 900.00 |
| Player's Favors: | | |
|     Mugs 120 @ $8 | 960.00 | |
|     Personalized Balls and Logo Markers | 240.00 | |
| Table Decorations | | 200.00 |
| Gratuities | | 100.00 |
| Film & Processing | | 20.00 |
| Postage | | <u>10.00</u> |
| | | |
| Total Projected Expenses | | $4,270.00 |

*Tournament Fee based on 120 players plus additional income from mulligan sales and "Drive by Pro" fee = $35.00 per person.*

## Job 43

| | |
|---|---|
| Barbara | Reg - 40, Overtime - 2 |
| Janie | Reg - 40, Overtime - 2-1/2 |
| Gene | Reg - 40, Overtime - 3 |
| (Yours) | Reg - 40, Overtime - 2 |
| Jack | Reg - 28 |

## Job 44

Quantities sold during the second week in May:

| Item | Quan | Item | Quan |
|---|---|---|---|
| 1027 | 5 | 1016 | 1 |
| 1004 | 3 | 1017 | 3 |
| 1007 | 3 | 1022 | 3 |
| 1011 | 3 | 1024 | 3 |
| 1012 | 1 | 1049 | 1 |
| 1015 | 1 | 1054 | 3 |

## Job 45

The meeting of the Par Fore Golf League Board Members was held at 1:00 pm, Tuesday, May (*first Tuesday*), (*year*), in the Club Room conducted by the league president, Barb Krull.

All members of the board of directors for the Par Fore Golf League were in attendance. Also attending the meeting were the co-chairpersons of the upcoming Invitational Tournament.

Alex Holbrook moved that the minutes of the April board meeting be approved as read. The motion was seconded and passed.

Margaret Dobe, treasurer, reported that the balance on hand was $2,105.53. The report was placed on file for audit.

The current membership of the Par Fore league is 54.

There have been no changes to the local rules.

New handicap cards are available every two weeks. Pick them up in the pro shop.

The outside tournaments listing will be posted on the bulletin board outside the pro shop. If more people sign up then there are slots available, a lotery will be held.

Twelve clubs were invited so that a total of 90 guests could attend. This leaves 30 slots open for Par Fore members.

The format for the tournament will be two best balls of the foursome.

The pro shop staff is working with tournament committee members to secure prizes for tournament. These prizes will be custom-made baskets.

The luncheon following the tournament will offer a choice of three entrees to be determined by the Chairperson and the club manager.

Sign-up sheets for volunteers have been posted in the pro shop. Volunteers are needed to help with registration, cart and golf bag arrangements, and table settings.

There was no old business.

**Suggested Minutes Layout**

There was no new business.

The next meeting will be held on the Tuesday prior to the Invitational Tournament at 1:00 pm in the Club Room.

The meeting was adjourned at 2:30 pm.

## *Job 47*

INVITATIONAL TOURNAMENT
Tuesday, July (first Tuesday), (year)

**Format**: 2 best balls of 4     **Registration**: 7:30-8:30 a.m. with coffee
**Fee**: $35 per person     **Shotgun Start**: 8:30 a.m.
**Handicap**: Maximum Handicap of 36, Handicap Index of 35.2 (90% of handicap will be used)
**Registration Deadline**: June 15, (year)

1. Fill in players' names, handicap, index, and menu selections. Check if carts are needed. Choose: Chicken Primavera (**CP**), Shrimp Primavera (**SP**), or Ham Steak w/pineapple (**HS**).
2. Make checks payable to P.F.G.L.
3. Amount Enclosed: _____ Number of Players at $35 each = $ _____
4. Return to Lynn Doell, 1011 Ballard Street, Cincinnati, OH 45209 (513-555-6797)

- - - - - - - - - - - - - - - - - - - - - - - - - - - - - - - - - - - - - - - - - - - - - - - - - - - - - - - - - - - - -

|  |  |  |  | Menu Selection | | |
| --- | --- | --- | --- | --- | --- | --- |
| **Name** | **Handicap** | **Index** | **Cart** | CP | SP | HS |
| 1. _____ | _____ | _____ | _____ | __ | __ | __ |
| 2. _____ | _____ | _____ | _____ | __ | __ | __ |

etc.

## *Job 48*

ATTENTION: OUTSIDE INVITATIONAL CHAIRPERSON

The Ohio River Golf Association cordially invites eight (8) members of your Golf Association to join us for our Fourth Annual Invitational Tournament to be held on Tuesday, June 4, 1996. The names of two alternate players are also requested.

Details for the tournament include:

    REGISTRATION — 8 a.m. (coffee and refreshments provided)

    TEE OFF TIME — 9 a.m., SHOTGUN Start

    ENTRY FEE — $35 per person (includes green fees, cart, refreshments, luncheon and prizes)

    FORMAT — Two best balls of four

    REQUIREMENT — Maximum handicap index of 35.2 (90% of handicap will be used.)

Please send your list of entrants with current handicap (maximum 36) and entry fees no later than May 1. No refunds will be made *after* May 15. An entry form is enclosed for your convenience. Get the name of your members in quickly. We will accept the first 90 entrants. If none of your members wishes to attend, please notify us as soon as possible.

We look forward to your participation. If there is any additional information that would be helpful to you, please contact us. Again, return your entry form with payment no later than May 1.

Sincerely,


Olga Christianson, Chairperson
(513) 555-2411

Enclosure


## Job 49

| Handicap | 90% Conversion |
|---|---|
| 1 | 0.9 |
| 2 | 1.8 |

etc.

## Job 50

| | |
|---|---|
| Barbara | Reg - 40, Overtime - 2 |
| Janie | Reg - 40, Overtime - 0 |
| Gene | Reg - 40, Overtime - 3 |
| (Yours) | Reg - 40, Overtime - 2 |
| Jack | Reg - 27 |

## Job 51

Quantities sold during the fourth week in May:

| Item | Quan | Item | Quan |
|---|---|---|---|
| 1027 | 2 | 1014 | 1 |
| 1028 | 2 | 1016 | 3 |
| 1002 | 1 | 1017 | 4 |
| 1004 | 1 | 1020 | 2 |
| 1006 | 2 | 1023 | 4 |
| 1009 | 2 | 1025 | 4 |
| 1010 | 1 | 1050 | 1 |
| 1012 | 3 | | |

## Job 53

| Acct. # | Item | Recipient | Amount |
|---|---|---|---|
| 3349 | phone note pads | Janie Hodges | $29.50 |
| 3348 | tape | Janie Hodges | $3.75 |
| 3349 | tacks | Janie Hodges | $4.29 |
| 3350 | 8-1/2" x 11" white card stock | Janie Hodges | $8.95 |

Job 54

# RANGERING

## SLOW PLAY, THE MAJOR PROBLEM FACING THE GOLF RANGER

A term used frequently throughout this handbook is "KEEPING PACE." It simply means playing at the rate of speed calculated to complete an 18 hole round in a four-hour time frame. Four hours is the generally accepted standard on most golf courses for an 18-hole round of golf.

This figure may vary somewhat depending on the length and difficulty of the course, but that variance will rarely exceed +/- 15 minutes. Assuming that the Starter directs groups to tee-off at 8-minute intervals, there will be 30 groups on the golf course at any given time. These 30 groups optimally represent a flow of 30 golfers per hour.

Remember that wasted time on the golf course means slower play and fewer players. slow play is the greatest single complaint of golfers. Consider this: one wasted minute on the golf course, per hole, can translate into 18 minutes of lost time for every group following the slow group. That can translate into 2½ fewer groups (optimally 10 golfers) on the course resulting in slow play for everyone.

**THE RANGER MUST RECOGNIZE SLOW PLAY**

Strange as it may seem, slow play may not be easily recognized. A fast golf swing, a fast walk, or a fast cart ride do not necesarily indicate a fast pace, nor does a slow swing necessarily reflect a slow pace. There should be a "timetable" for each hole on the course. Very often, the "timetable" of elapsed times is printed on the course scorecard. The ranger should be familiar with the number of minutes required to reach a certain point on the course and estimate whether players are keeping pace. In addition to the timing, the ranger should be able to judge whether the pace is being maintained by the intervals between groups.

If a group is playing faster that the "specs" indicate, there could be a longer than normal interval between the fast playing group and the following group. Slow play could be mistakenly "called" when a group consisting of low-handicap, long hitters may seem to wait an inordinately long time before hitting drives or second shots. The key words and the key thought here is "OUT OF RANGE"; meaning that the group on the tee may drive when the preceding group is "OUT OF THEIR RANGE" and not necessarily after the leading group has hit subsequent shots.

**SLOW PLAY HAS MANY CAUSES**

The reasons can be summed up very easily: wasted strokes and wasted time. The ranger should be aware that a limited number of strokes should be taken on a hole when groups of following golfers are being delayed. A practical rule of thumb could be the following: On par 3 holes, 3 strokes up to the green; on par 4 holes, 5 strokes up to the green; on par 5 holes, 6 strokes up to the green. A maxamum of 4 putts should be allowed; if, by that time, the player has not holed out, he or she should be instructed to pick up his ball and move on to the next hole.

Concerning "wasted time", there are several areas where the "devil" of wasted time frequently rears his ugly head. The first one is on the tee. Players should be encouraged to hit as soon as the preceding group is out of range, rather then waiting before (a) approaching the tee; (b) deciding the hitting order; (c) deciding which club to use; (d) taking practice swings; (e) deciding on the "right" teeing spot.

The second most serious area of wasted time is balls landing or rolling in the rough. Many slow golfers hit the ball and immediately start to walk to their golf bags to put away their club. The 3 or 4 seconds spent watching the flight and the roll of the ball will pay handsome dividends when it comes to locating a ball for the next shot.

More time is wasted on the green than any other place on the course. Deciding who is "away"; lining up the shot from every conceivable angle; excessive practice stroking all contribute to slow play. Those "exercises" should not be tollerated if any hope of a 4 hour pace is to be maintained.

**WHAT CAN THE RANGER DO ABOUT TIME CONSUMING WASTED STROKES AND TOO MUCH WASTED TIME?**

**First, he or she must be visible.** Most golfers know why a ranger is monitering the course. When a group is taking to many strokes and holding up play, approach them and ask them to please pick up the pace. Its acceptible, if after being asked to pick up the pace without any discernible acceleration, for the ranger to ask them, in a pleasent way, to pick up the ball(s) and move to the next hole.

On the course, and whenever possible, the ranger should watch the flight and roll of balls. By so doing, he or she may be able to assist in locating an erant ball for the golfer.

Golfers should be encouraged to postpone the "high-fives" and "victory dancing" until they vacate the green. They should be instructed to park their carts and other gear away from the enterance to the green. In addition, they should be encouraged to vacate the green as soon as they hole out or pick up. Scores should be recorded away from the greens.

## *Job 55*

CHECKLIST
PAR FORE INVITATIONAL TOURNAMENT

Activities to be Completed                                                                 Completed

Correspondence
    Announcement Letter (6 weeks before tournament)         _____
    Letter of Invitation (4 weeks before tournament)         _____
    Thank-you letters                                         _____
    Other _____                     _____
Lists
    Participants by Club                                      _____
    Alphabetic List of Participants with Hole Assignments     _____
    Foursomes by Hole                                         _____
    Handicap Sheet Showing 90% Conversion                     _____
Volunteers
    Registration (3)                                          _____
    Sell Mulligans (1)                                        _____
    Sell Tickets for Money Trees (2)                          _____
    Cart Organization and Bag Handling (6 men)                _____
    Cart Favor Organization and Distribution (2)              _____
    Table Decorations—Make and Set Up (Sue Staude, chairperson) _____
    Other _____                     _____
Preparations
    PFGL Sign-up Sheet (4 weeks before tournament)            _____
    Morning Treat Sign-up Sheet                               _____
    Mulligans (Cut out)                                       _____

    Money Trees (make 2)
    Tournament Rules Sheet (Prepare, have checked, copy, 1 per cart)
    Special Events Sheet (prepare, copy, distribute at registration)
    Score Cards per Foursome
    Other _____
Supplies
    Poster Board
    Name tags, pens, misc.
    Other _____
Food Functions
    Function Sheet
        Luncheon Menu
        Morning Coffee/Tea Set-up
        Snack at the turn
        Room Set-up
    Other _____

## Job 56

SUBJECT: Sponsorship of Par Fore Golf League Annual Invitational Tournament

The Sixth Annual Invitational Golf Tournament will be held on July (first Tuesday), (current year), at the Ohio River Golf Club hosted by the Par Fore Golf League. There will be 120 participants representing 12 clubs from around the Cincinnati area.

Each year we invite local car dealerships to sponsor our Hole-in-One event, and each year we have been fortunate enough to have a sponsor for one of our Par 3 holes. The sponsorship consists of donating one of your subcompact cars as the prize for the first person in the tournament to make a hole-in-one on a specific hole. In return for your sponsorship, your dealership will be recognized during registration with a table display thanking you along with any promotional material you would like us to exhibit. In addition, a sign designating your sponsorship will be posted on the respective hole, and your dealership will be recognized and thanked again at the tournament luncheon. Any publicity of this event will also include your involvement.

```
Feister Ford, Inc.
1224 Ridge Road
Cincinnati, OH 45227

Valette Chevrolet
9292 Montgomery Road
Montgomery, OH 45242

Norwood Chrysler
2130 Cameron Avenue
Norwood, OH 45212
```

May we count on you this year to sponsor the most exciting event of the tournament? We will be calling you next week for your answer. In the meantime, if you have any questions, please call me at the number below my name, or call the Pro Shop at the Ohio River Golf Club.

We look forward to a successful tournament made more special with your involvement.

## Job 58—Pro Shop Checklist

DETAILS WITH PRO SHOP STAFF
~~BOGEY BUDDIES~~ INVITATIONAL TOURNAMENT *(fix)*
~~July (first Tuesday), (year)~~ *(fix)*

| | Completed |
|---|---|
| Activities to be Completed | |
| Need to Order | |
|     Mugs for favors (120 @ $6.50 ea. or less) | _____ |
|     Logo Balls (10 dozen @ $10 per doz.) | _____ |
|     Tees and Ball Markers (120 each; $12 total) | _____ |

Preparation
    Registration Table
    Roll of Tickets with Stubs for Money Tree
    Score Board   (Cart Signs)
    ^Practice Balls available on Driving Range
    Special Event Holes
        Closest to the Pin #7—Guest   #16
        Closest to the Pin ~~#14~~—Member   #14
        Closest to the Line ~~#16~~—Guest
        Closest to the Line #5—Member
        Longest Drive #9—entire field

Prizes
    Custom-made baskets for top ~~2~~ 3 teams (12 at $20 each)
    Member prizes—Closest to Hole, Straightest Drive
        Certificates for Round of Golf for 4 at ~~Black Diamond~~ River View
    Guest prizes—Closest to Hole, Straightest Drive
        Certificates for Round of Golf for 4 at ~~Chaske~~ Ohio River
    (Longest) ~~Straightest~~ Drive—Par Fore Golf Towel and Balls
    Hole-in-One (?)

Tournament Assistance
    Post Scores to Score Board
    Determine Winners
    Prepare Redeemable Certificates for Tournament Winners
    Other _____

## Job 59

| | |
|---|---|
| Barbara | Reg - 40, Overtime - 2 |
| Janie | Reg - 40, Overtime - 1 |
| Gene | Reg - 40, Overtime - 0 |
| (Yours) | Reg - 40, Overtime - 1-1/2 |
| Jack | Reg - 25 |

## Job 60

Quantities sold during the second week in June:

| Item | Quan | Item | Quan |
|---|---|---|---|
| 1027 | 3 | 1015 | 2 |
| 1001 | 1 | 1016 | 1 |
| 1004 | 2 | 1017 | 1 |
| 1009 | 1 | 1026 | 1 |
| 1010 | 2 | 1054 | 3 |
| 1011 | 4 | | |

Source Documents

## Job 61

July 4, 1994

Dear Member:

Based on our ongoing efforts to make golf at Bridgemoore more enjoyable for all players, the golf association at Bridgemoore intends to implement a program that we feel will contribute to this end result.

Our golf course has been evaluated, and it is felt that the average player should be able to play the Bridgemoore course in 4 hours or less. This evaluation was based on the course layout, difficulty of holes, distance between holes, etc. Currently, our time, on average, is slightly over 4 hours, which is not far off target. Unfortunately, there are days when part of the field is finished in 4 hours and others are closer to 5 hours. It would appear that these delays are caused by slow players who are unaware of the problems they create or are inconsiderate of their fellow members. We would like to improve this condition of slow play for the betterment of all members by introducing the following procedures.

The Bridgemoore owners have agreed to pay a ranger who will report directly to a committee of selected members from the Bridgemoore Association. The ranger, along with committee members, will try to better identify where flow problems develop as well as other possible reasons for slow play. We will have an ongoing program in which informative tapes will be shown on WPKR. Thse tapes will be supplied by the USGA and will focus on golf etiquete, course management, etc. We have many new golfers who might benefit from this instruction, along with more experienced golfers who might gain from a refresher course.

Important to this program is Mr. John Johnson, who was interviewed and hired by Bridgemoore to function as ranger. John has had experience at other clubs and comes highly recommended by his previous employers. He will be responsible for assisting play in a courteous, diplomatic, constructive manner which should benefit us all. Please meet and greet John when he assumes his responsibilities in the near future.

Remember, please, that this is a collective, constructive effort to make our golfing experience more enjoyable for all and not an effort to embarrass the slow player. We hope this program will be educational for all of us in identifying areas in which each of us might improve our games. Overall, this program will contribute to the targeted 4-hour round we can all enjoy.

We have included a copy of selected pages from the *Golf Vollunteer's Handbook*, which you might find interesting. It would appear we are not alone in our slow play dilemma. We have supplied John Johnson with the complete booklet as a guideline for his activities.

We would appreciate your help and cooperation in implementing this effort, and if you have any thoughts as to how it might be improved, contact your Bridgmoore Association Board or the Bridgemoore pro shop.

Thank you!

## Job 63

NOTICE!!

Due to the tremendous response to the (year) Invitational Golf Tournament, we ask that you notify either Lynn Doell or Florence Rogers if you will be unable to play in the tournament on July (insert first Wednesday).

Please DO NOT cross your name off the sign-up sheet. The slots will be given to the signed alternates in the order of signing.

In order to be considered officially registered for the tournament, you will need to pay your registration fee ($35) no later than June 15 unless you have made other arrangements with one of the tournament chairpersons. Missing this deadline will result in your name being removed from the participants' list to the list of alternates.

Alternates will be notified no later than June 22 if an opening is available due to cancellation or non-payment. Also, alternates will be called to fill any last-minute cancellations.

Thank you for your cooperation.

(Include co-chairpersons names and phone numbers.)

## Job 64

**Guests**

| NAME | CLUB | Food | HCP | 90% | HOLE # |
|---|---|---|---|---|---|
| Archdekin, Margaret | Seven Hills | HS | 27 | 24.3 | 14B |
| Armstrong, Babs | River View | SP | 29 | 26.1 | 9A |
| Ashton, Ann | Glenview | CP | 23 | 20.7 | 6A |
| Aylward, Karl | Sharon Woods | SP | 30 | 27 | 2A |
| Bernklau, Dolores | Brooksville | CP | 35 | 31.5 | 8B |
| Boluch, Joyce | Sharon Woods | SP | 29 | 26.1 | 8B |
| Bowles, Jay | Oak Hills | CP | 34 | 30.6 | 10A |
| Bowles, Zelma | Delhi Hills | CP | 22 | 19.8 | 18A |
| Boyle, Marie | Brooksville | HS | 25 | 22.5 | 15B |
| Burnley, John | Seven Rivers | HS | 28 | 25.2 | 13 |
| Butler, Sylvia | Seville | CP | 27 | 24.3 | 16 |
| Callahan, Claire | Brooksville | CP | 25 | 22.5 | 15A |
| Calnan, Connie | Delhi Hills | SP | 36 | 32.4 | 5B |
| Carlson, Pam | Black Diamond | SP | 25 | 22.5 | 17A |
| Colby, Mark | Glenview | CP | 18 | 16.2 | 6B |
| Colmery, Judy | Seville | SP | 19 | 17.1 | 9B |
| Condon, Marion | Seven Hills | SP | 33 | 29.7 | 17B |
| Craib, May | Brooksville | SP | 26 | 23.4 | 2A |
| Cunningham, Jean | Sharon Woods | CP | 20 | 18 | 12A |
| Dittmar, Corbie | Oak Hills | CP | 24 | 21.6 | 9A |
| Doane, Jinny | Delhi Hills | HS | 27 | 24.3 | 15B |
| Dougan, Dolly | Black Diamond | SP | 28 | 25.2 | 18A |
| Downey, Jean | Brooksville | SP | 21 | 18.9 | 15A |
| Dunstan, Earl | Seven Hills | CP | 26 | 23.4 | 1A |
| Edmunds, Sue | Seville | CP | 24 | 21.6 | 10A |
| Ellis, Sam | Black Diamond | SP | 15 | 13.5 | 4 |
| Ephraim, Peg | Sharon Woods | SP | 9 | 8.1 | 1B |
| Feihl, Ida | River View | SP | 33 | 29.7 | 15B |
| Ferrari, Lee | Silver Springs | CP | 36 | 32.4 | 3 |
| Garippo, Dean | Delhi Hills | SP | 31 | 27.9 | 2B |
| Gravely, Barbara | Oak Hills | SP | 33 | 29.7 | 15A |
| Hadsell, Don | River View | CP | 33 | 29.7 | 12A |
| Harris, Bette | Silver Springs | CP | 30 | 27 | 8A |

| | | | | | |
|---|---|---|---|---|---|
| Harris, Neal | Oak Hills | HS | 24 | 21.6 | 12B |
| Holbrook, Mary Lou | Glenview | CP | 20 | 18 | 13 |
| James, Patty | Glenview | SP | 22 | 19.8 | 17B |
| Katke, Betty | Brooksville | SP | 30 | 27 | 4 |
| King, Elsie | Seville | SP | 26 | 23.4 | 1B |
| Koclanes, Lucky | Silver Springs | CP | 20 | 18 | 13 |
| Koenig, Lillian | Oak Hills | CP | 28 | 25.2 | 10B |
| Langrock, Paula | Sharon Woods | HS | 30 | 27 | 2B |
| LaVell, Frank | Silver Springs | CP | 22 | 19.8 | 17A |
| LeVert, Penny | Seven Rivers | SP | 36 | 32.4 | 5A |
| Malby, Shirley | Chaska | CP | 22 | 19.8 | 18A |
| Marshall, Corey | River View | CP | 18 | 16.2 | 8A |
| Martin, Rose | Delhi Hills | CP | 26 | 23.4 | 4 |
| Maxwell, Val | Chaska | SP | 33 | 29.7 | 14A |
| McCarty, Maggie | Silver Springs | CP | 22 | 19.8 | 9B |
| McKersie, Ann | Black Diamond | SP | 18 | 16.2 | 8B |
| Miedaner, Raymond | Silver Springs | HS | 30 | 27 | 7 |
| Minear, David | Black Diamond | SP | 23 | 20.7 | 7 |
| Murray, Barbara | Glenview | SP | 28 | 25.2 | 12B |
| Nardone, Shirley | Seven Rivers | CP | 30 | 27 | 18B |
| Nelles, Dot | Chaska | CP | 24 | 21.6 | 12A |
| O'Neil, Kay | Glenview | HS | 19 | 17.1 | 10B |
| Oriel, Priscilla | Chaska | CP | 25 | 22.5 | 17B |
| Outhouse, Dave | Seven Rivers | SP | 33 | 29.7 | 14B |
| Peacock, Mary Lou | Chaska | SP | 17 | 15.3 | 6A |
| Perlman, Aggie | River View | CP | 34 | 30.6 | 9A |
| Pomeroy, Judy | Delhi Hills | CP | 32 | 28.8 | 16 |
| Puglise, Frank | River View | CP | 29 | 26.1 | 6A |
| Samuelson, Hiram | Brooksville | SP | 22 | 19.8 | 7 |
| Schulz, Phyllis | Glenview | SP | 28 | 25.2 | 11 |
| Sefranek, Helen | Black Diamond | HS | 16 | 14.4 | 5A |
| Sequin, Marion | Seven Hills | SP | 29 | 26.1 | 5B |
| Shaw, Elaine | Seven Hills | CP | 23 | 20.7 | 8A |
| Shook, Joanne | Oak Hills | SP | 25 | 22.5 | 1B |
| Sinclair, Jan | Seven Rivers | SP | 30 | 27 | 1A |
| Smith, Helen | Seven Hills | HS | 24 | 21.6 | 14A |
| Sutch, Eddie | Oak Hills | SP | 31 | 27.9 | 6B |
| Thompson, Patrick | Black Diamond | HS | 14 | 12.6 | 3 |
| Thurnherr, Steve | Sharon Woods | CP | 25 | 22.5 | 18B |
| Trowbridge, Denise | Black Diamond | SP | 11 | 9.9 | 2B |
| Tuttle, Bill | Seven Hills | CP | 25 | 22.5 | 18B |
| Vaseleniuck, Maura | Chaska | CP | 16 | 14.4 | 5B |
| Vermette, Hazel | Seville | CP | 20 | 18 | 14B |
| Wallace, Lyle | Silver Springs | CP | 19 | 17.1 | 11 |
| Walsh, Micky | Seville | CP | 29 | 26.1 | 5A |
| Walter, Lori | River View | SP | 29 | 26.1 | 6B |
| Weber, Joanne | Delhi Hills | CP | 28 | 25.2 | 10A |
| Welsh, Fran | Seville | SP | 25 | 22.5 | 16 |
| Whitcomb, Betty | Oak Hills | CP | 25 | 22.5 | 3 |
| Whitmore, Gene | Sharon Woods | HS | 28 | 25.2 | 9B |
| Wieczoreck, Lee | Seven Rivers | CP | 23 | 20.7 | 11 |
| Wilcox, Polly | Delhi Hills | SP | 32 | 28.8 | 17A |
| Williams, Sue | Chaska | SP | 24 | 21.6 | 10B |
| Woods, Scott | Chaska | CP | 29 | 26.1 | 2A |
| Yerxa, Carol Anne | Seven Rivers | SP | 27 | 24.3 | 12B |
| York, Gayle | Brooksville | SP | 36 | 32.4 | 1A |
| Zysek, Bob | Seven Rivers | HS | 27 | 24.3 | 14A |

**Par Fore Participants**

| Name | Hole | Hcp | Food | Name | Hole | Hcp | Food |
|---|---|---|---|---|---|---|---|
| Janine Anderson | 10B | 22 | CP | Louis Mitchell | 8A | 18 | CP |
| Owen Anderson | 1B | 17 | HS | Lillian Mitchell | 8B | 21 | CP |
| Bob Arndt | 14A | 29 | HS | Phoebe Phillips | 7 | 16 | SP |
| Margot Babcock | 15A | 14 | CP | Leslie Rogers | 12B | 19 | CP |
| Dave Brantley | 15B | 20 | HS | Florence Rogers | 1A | 10 | CP |
| Nancy Brantley | 4 | 24 | CP | Beulah Seager | 14B | 10 | HS |
| Dorothy Charles | 2A | 29 | SP | Christine Seitz | 17A | 20 | SP |
| Nancy Christianson | 6B | 21 | SP | Eugene Selle | 18A | 22 | HS |
| Margaret Dobbe | 17B | 23 | HS | Dennis Staples | 5B | 29 | CP |
| Lynn Doell | 3 | 30 | CP | Gloria Staples | 9B | 22 | CP |
| Peggy Eick | 5A | 27 | SP | Sue Staude | 9A | 25 | HS |
| Alex Holbrook | 12A | 23 | CP | Sue Steiner | 18B | 19 | SP |
| Kay Ihlenfeld | 2B | 27 | CP | Nancy Thiex | 10A | 16 | SP |
| Sue Jacobson | 11 | 24 | SP | John Van Alsteen | 6A | 11 | SP |
| Kay Koclanes | 16 | 25 | HS | Jean Van Alsteen | 13 | 30 | SP |

*Job 67*

PLEASE READ THIS NOTICE!

The following Par Fore members will be participating in the (year) Invitational Tournament on July (first Tuesday). Please arrive at **7:30 a.m.** so that cart assignments can be arranged.

*Job 69*

WELCOME to the (year)
Bogey Buddies Invitational Tournament
RULES AND INFORMATION

1. USGA Rules shall govern all play. Fourteen (14) Club Rule applies.
2. Play the ball as it lies. (The two best balls must be putted out.)
3. Play embedded ball rule through the green. (If ball is embedded, it may be cleaned and redropped with no penalty.)
4. Lateral Hazard--#9 marked by red lines.
5. Water Hazard--#1 and #9 marked by yellow lines. Ball must be played across the water without any drop.
6. All "ground under repair" marked with white lines.
7. You may sole your club in transition area (waste bunkers with pampas grass). You may not sole your club in sand traps.
8. Please repair all ball marks; rake sand traps; and fill divots with sand carried on your carts.
9. Please keep pace with the group in front of you--we want everyone to have fun!

---

SPECIAL EVENTS
Closest to the Pin
    Hole #7 (Guest)
    Hole #16 (Member)

Closest to the Line
    Hole #5 (Member)
    Hole #14 (Guest)

Longest Drive
    Hole #9 (All participants)

Hole in One?

*Source Documents*

Mulligans
> May be purchased at Registration ($1 each)
> Maximum of two (2)--one per nine holes
> You may substitute a mulligan for any shot from tee TO green (except on Special Event holes listed above). Mulligans may not be used on the green!

Ties
> All ties will be broken on a match of scorecards from the #1 handicap hole.

Have a great game!
> Co-chairpersons Lynn Doell and Florence Rogers

## Job 73

| | |
|---|---|
| Barbara | Reg - 40, Overtime - 2 |
| Janie | Reg - 40, Overtime - 3 |
| Gene | Reg - 40, Overtime - 2 |
| (Yours) | Reg - 40, Overtime - 4 |
| Jack | Reg - 30 |

## Job 74

Quantities sold during the fourth week in June:

| Item | Quan | Item | Quan |
|---|---|---|---|
| 1027 | 2 | 1015 | 4 |
| 1001 | 2 | 1016 | 2 |
| 1002 | 1 | 1017 | 6 |
| 1003 | 1 | 1021 | 4 |
| 1005 | 1 | 1023 | 1 |
| 1007 | 1 | 1025 | 1 |
| 1009 | 2 | 1046 | 1 |
| 1011 | 3 | 1054 | 2 |
| 1012 | 2 | 1061 | 1 |
| 1014 | 3 | | |

## Job 77

Create the following signs:

REGISTRATION
MULLIGANS
SPONSORS' RECOGNITION TABLE
WELCOME
RAFFLE TICKETS (Money Tree)

Suggested Sign Layout

*Job 78*

| Hole 1 | Par 4 | Depth 25 |
| Hole 2 | Par 4 | Depth 27 |
| Hole 3 | Par 4 | Depth 26 |
| Hole 4 | Par 3 | Depth 30 |
| Hole 5 | Par 5 | Depth 26 |
| Hole 6 | Par 4 | Depth 31 |
| Hole 7 | Par 3 | Depth 32 |
| Hole 8 | Par 4 | Depth 37 |
| Hole 9 | Par 5 | Depth 38 |
| Hole 10 | Par 4 | Depth 37 |
| Hole 11 | Par 3 | Depth 36 |
| Hole 12 | Par 4 | Depth 32 |
| Hole 13 | Par 5 | Depth 28 |
| Hole 14 | Par 4 | Depth 26 |
| Hole 15 | Par 4 | Depth 40 |
| Hole 16 | Par 3 | Depth 26 |
| Hole 17 | Par 4 | Depth 28 |
| Hole 18 | Par 5 | Depth 32 |

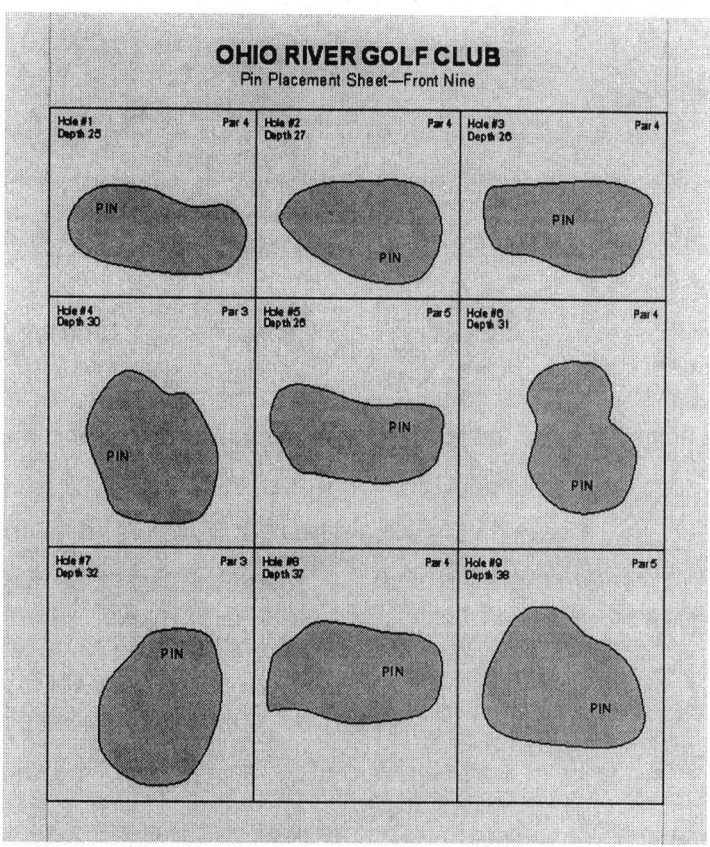

Pin Placement Sheet for the Front Nine

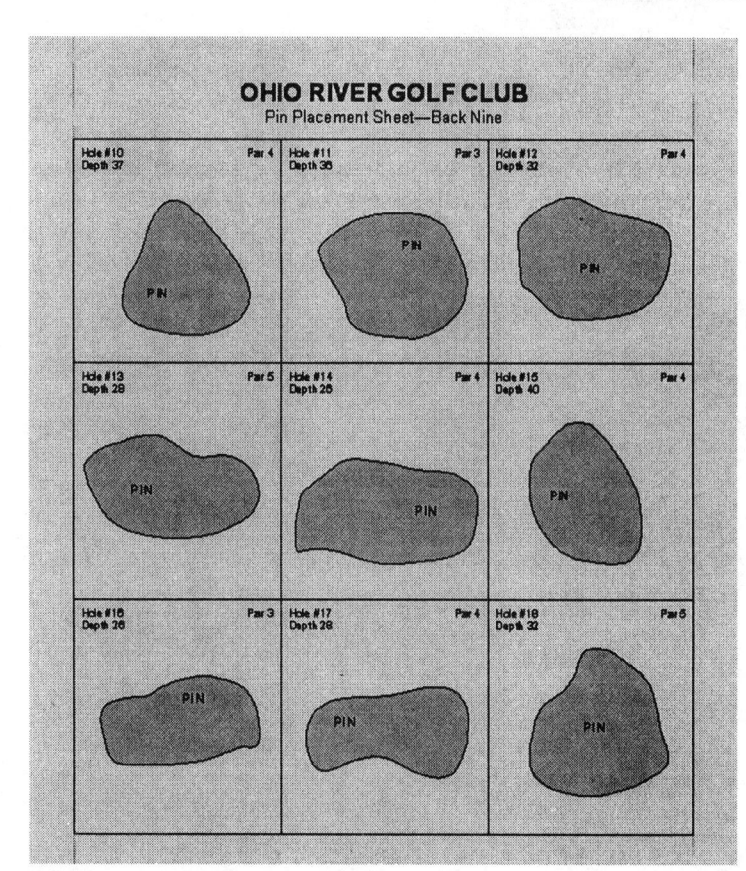

Pin Placement Sheet for the Back Nine

*Source Documents*

## Job 79

| Winners | | | Score |
|---|---|---|---|
| 1st | $60 each | Jacobson, Schulz, Wallace, Wieczoreck | 120 |
| 2nd | $50 each | Aylward, Charles, Craib, Woods | 123 |
| 3rd | $45 each | Armstrong, Dittmar, Perlman, Staude | 125 |
| 4th | $40 each | Buttler, Koclanes, Pomeroy, Welsh | 126 |
| 5th | $35 each | Nardone, Steiner, Thurnherr, Tuttle | 128 |
| 6th | $30 each | Miedaner, Minear, Phillips, Samuelson | 128 |
| 7th | $25 each | Archdekin, Outhouse, Seager, Vermette | 129 |
| 8th | $20 each | Garippo, Ihlenfeld, Langrock, Trowbridge | 131 |

Each member of the top three teams also receives a custom-made basket.

Closest to the Pin
    Hole #7    Dot Nelles, Chaska    Gift certificate for a round of golf for 4 at Ohio River
    Hole #16    Peggy Eick, Par Fore    Gift certificate for a round of golf for 4 at River View

Closest to the Line
    Hole #5    Leslie Rogers, Par Fore    Gift certificate for a round of golf for 4 at River View
    Hole #14    Earl Dunstan, Seven Hills    Gift certificate for a round of golf for 4 at Ohio River

Longest Drive
    Hole #9    Frank LaVell, Silver Springs    Ohio River balls and towel

Hole-in-One    None

## Job 80

Use any border and any fonts available to create attractive certificates.

*Par Fore League Invitational Tournament*
*at the Ohio River Golf Club*
*Cincinnati, Ohio*

This is to certify that

Sue Jacobson

Placed FIRST
July (first Tuesday), (year)

_____        _____
Tournament Chairperson                           Date

Suggestion for Certificate

*Job 81*

AGENDA
PAR FORE BOARD MEETING

JULY (second Tuesday), (year)
1:00 p.m. Club Room

CALL TO ORDER . . . . . . . . . . . . . . . . . . . . . . . . . . . . . . . . . . . . . . . . . . . . . . . . . . . . . . . . (President)
READING OF MINUTES . . . . . . . . . . . . . . . . . . . . . . . . . . . . . . . . . . . . . . . . . . . . . . . . . . (Secretary)
TREASURER'S REPORT . . . . . . . . . . . . . . . . . . . . . . . . . . . . . . . . . . . . . . . . . . . . . . . . . . (Treasurer)
COMMITTEE REPORTS:
    Membership . . . . . . . . . . . . . . . . . . . . . . . . . . . . . . . . . . . . . . . . (Membership Chairperson)
    Rules . . . . . . . . . . . . . . . . . . . . . . . . . . . . . . . . . . . . . . . . . . . . . . . . . . . (Rules Chairperson)
    Handicap . . . . . . . . . . . . . . . . . . . . . . . . . . . . . . . . . . . . . . . . . . . . . (Handicap Chairperson)
    Tournaments . . . . . . . . . . . . . . . . . . . . . . . . . . . . . . . . . . . . . . . . (Tournament Chairperson)
        Invitational Tournament . . . . . . . . . . . . . . . . . . . . . . . . . . . . (Invitational Co-Chairperson)
OLD BUSINESS . . . . . . . . . . . . . . . . . . . . . . . . . . . . . . . . . . . . . . . . . . . . . . . . . . . . . . . . . (President)
NEW BUSINESS . . . . . . . . . . . . . . . . . . . . . . . . . . . . . . . . . . . . . . . . . . . . . . . . . . . . . . . . (President)
ADJOURNMENT

*Job 82*

Income:
Registration Fees       120 @ $35

Expenses:
Luncheon       120 @ $8.50
Snack     $120.00
Coffee/Tea     $100.00
Cart Fee for Guests    60 @ $5
Prizes (Pro Shop Gift Certificates)    $900
Mugs, Logo Balls, Tees and Ball Markers    $941.60
Table Decorations    $178.88
Film & Processing    $22.45
Postage  $6.20
Gratuities    $100.00

*Job 83—Minutes of Board Meeting*

The meeting of the Par Fore Golf League Board Members was held at 1:00 pm, Tuesday, July (second Tuesday), (year), in the Club Room conducted by the league president, Barb Krull.

All members of the board of directors for the Par Fore Golf League were in attendance. Also attending the meeting were the chairpersons of the Invitational Tournament.

Peggy Eick moved that the minutes of last week's meeting be approved as read. The motion was seconded and passed.

Margaret Dobbe, treasurer, reported that the balance on hand was $1,245.72. The report was placed on file for audit.

The current membership remains at 54.

The rules chairman asks members to remind their guests that Ohio River Golf Club is a "soft spikes" facility.

**Source Documents**

Our course will undergo a study to examine the existing hole handicaps. Members are reminded to "hole out" each hole and put actual scores on scorecards. Adjustments will be made by pro shop staff.

We have received five notices from other clubs for their invitational tournaments. All notices have been posted on the bulletin board outside the pro shop.

The Invitational Tournament was a great success. Tournament chairpersons thanked all the board members and other volunteers for their help. There were 120 participants in the tournament. A copy of the financial statement detailing the income and expenses of the tournament was handed out to each board member.

There was no old business.

There was no new business.

The next meeting will be held on the Tuesday at 1:00 pm in the Club Room prior to the Closing Day luncheon.

The meeting adjourned at 2:15 p.m.

## Job 84

| | |
|---|---|
| Barbara | Reg - 40, Overtime - 0 |
| Janie | Reg - 40, Overtime - 1 |
| Gene | Reg - 40, Overtime - 0 |
| (Yours) | Reg - 40, Overtime - 0 |
| Jack | Reg - 24 |

## Job 85

Quantities sold during the second week in July:

| Item | Quan | Item | Quan |
|---|---|---|---|
| 1027 | 1 | 1015 | 3 |
| 1028 | 3 | 1016 | 1 |
| 1001 | 1 | 1017 | 8 |
| 1004 | 2 | 1023 | 2 |
| 1005 | 4 | 1025 | 2 |
| 1006 | 4 | 1049 | 1 |
| 1011 | 3 | 1050 | 1 |
| 1012 | 2 | 1054 | 3 |
| 1013 | 1 | | |

## Job 89

| | |
|---|---|
| Barbara | Reg - 40, Overtime - 2 |
| Janie | Reg - 40, Overtime - 3 |
| Gene | Reg - 40, Overtime - 1 |
| (Yours) | Reg - 40, Overtime - 3 |
| Jack | Reg - 26 |

## Job 90

Quantities sold during the fourth week in July:

| Item | Quan | Item | Quan |
|---|---|---|---|
| 1027 | 2 | 1016 | 3 |
| 1001 | 1 | 1017 | 4 |
| 1002 | 2 | 1020 | 3 |
| 1005 | 4 | 1022 | 3 |
| 1006 | 6 | 1024 | 3 |
| 1009 | 1 | 1026 | 1 |
| 1011 | 2 | 1049 | 1 |
| 1012 | 1 | 1054 | 5 |
| 1014 | 2 | 1061 | 1 |
| 1015 | 1 | | |